ESSENTIALLY
Eggplant

Nina Kehayan

FISHER
BOOKS™

Publishers: Bill Fisher
Howard Fisher
Helen V. Fisher

North American Helen V. Fisher
Editors: Sarah Smith

Cover Design: FifthStreetdesign
Cover Illustration: Nicci Walker
Illustrations: Nicci Walker
Book Design: Deanie Wood
Nutrient Analysis: Miriam Fisher
Recipe Adaptation: Helen V. Fisher

First published in the English
language by Grub Street,
London, England
First published by
Editions de l'aube, France
English language translation
© Heather Maxwell 1995
© Grub Street 1995
Americanized version
© Fisher Books 1996

Library of Congress Cataloging-in-
Publication Data

Kehayan, Nina, 1946-
Essentially eggplant / Nina
Kehayan.
p. cm.
Includes bibliographical
references and index.
ISBN 1-55561-1117
1. Cookery (Eggplant) 2.
Cookery, International. 3.
Onions.
I. Title.
TX803.E4K45 1996
641.6'5646--dc20   96-34444
CIP

North American Edition
Published by Fisher Books
4239 W. Ina Road, Suite #101
Tucson, AZ 85741
(520) 744-6110

Printed in USA
Printing 10 9 8 7 6 5 4 3 2 1

ii

Contents

Foreword

The eggplant has long been a source of fascination. In striking contrast to our leeks and cabbages, carrots and cauliflower, it seems to promise all the exotic charms of the Far and Middle East. Its bland and subtle flesh readily absorbs all the flavors of a Turkish spice market, while its texture can be rendered crisp and tender by frying, or melting and mellow by baking.

Those of us who were growing up just after the war remember the reappearance of the eggplant, and the excitement it engendered. Yet eggplants had been around, on and off, for some three hundred years. The first variety to reach our shores was probably the pearly-white egg-shaped form, which gave rise to the name eggplant, by which it is still known in the US. By Victorian times, the white eggplant was believed to be unhealthful, but was still being cultivated for decorative purposes. Others grown with the same aim included a spectacular round jet-black globe called Perkin Black.

Nina Kehayan and her parents, her husband and his parents, like the wandering Jews of legend, made their separate ways across Europe after having been driven out of their homes in Russia, Poland and Armenia. They settled finally in France: Nina's family in Paris, her husband's in Marseilles. Eventually the young couple met, married, and made their home in Provence.

I can understand the author's affectionate claim that Provence is the natural home of the eggplant, for it is her home also and she knows it far better than I. But for me it will always be associated most strongly with Turkey, for it was here that I first learned to love it. The eggplant is very much a part of the Turkish cuisine, and fits naturally into their meal pattern and way of life. The fierce dry heat of the brazier and grill is ideal for roasting eggplants, while the inimitable Turkish yogurt blends exquisitely with them.

Eggplant dishes are legion in Turkey: smoky purées laced with garlic and sharpened with lemon juice; baked dishes of eggplants and tomatoes, layered with herbs; whole eggplants stuffed with ground lamb, or with rice and herbs, or bulgur wheat.

Many years ago, at a dinner based on eggplants, in an old wooden house overlooking the Bosphorus, I first heard the story of the foreign guest who asked for a glass of water after his meal: "just plain water, if you please, without eggplant. . . ."

Arabella Boxer

Acknowledgments

Most sincere thanks are extended to all those who kindly lent me their expertise, whether artistic, linguistic or gastronomic, philosophical or technical.

Many comments, suggestions and recipes were sent to me by readers of the first edition of this work and they have given me considerable assistance in producing this edition. In particular, I wish to mention: Madame Marion Nazet, President of the La Couqueto Club in Marseilles; Monsieur Setrak Ettarian, chef, Le Chiraz Restaurant, Marseilles; and the Tchakalian brothers, of the TCH oriental grocery in Marseilles.

Nutrient Analysis

Nutrient analysis was calculated using The Food Processor® for Windows software program, version 6.0, copyright 1987-1995 by ESHA Research.

Analysis does not include optional ingredients or variations. Where an ingredient amount is a range, the higher number is used. Where the number of servings is a range, the lower number is used. Unless specified otherwise in the recipe, 2% milk was assumed in all recipes using milk.

The following abbreviations are used:

Cal = Calories
Prot = Protein
Carb = Carbohydrates
Fib = Fiber
Tot. Fat = Total Fat
Sat. Fat = Saturated Fat
Chol = Cholesterol

Introduction

Did you know the eggplant is not a vegetable at all? Technically, it's a fruit—a berry, to be exact. It belongs to the nightshade family, which means it is related to the tomato, potato, tobacco and petunia.

No matter; the eggplant is undeniably beautiful. Its shiny patent-leather skin is most often deep purple, but it also comes in shades of lavender, white, red, green and yellow, in solid colors or stripes. Some eggplants are the size of small watermelons; others as small as marbles. Their shape can be round, oval, pear-shaped, long and thin or short and fat.

The eggplant has a wonderfully subtle flavor and a dense texture. It absorbs and enhances the flavor of other ingredients while adding a smooth richness to the dish. It is low in calories and high in potassium and fiber. It also provides some folate, magnesium and phosphorus. A 4-ounce serving contains 32 calories.

A popular method in many cuisines is to cook eggplant whole and then chop or purée the flesh and combine it with other ingredients. It can be cooked in the oven, but traditionally it is roasted in its skin over a gas flame or an outdoor grill, giving the flesh an exciting smoky tang.

Eggplant caviar is a thick, puréed mixture of roasted eggplant, oil and various other ingredients and seasonings. It is found in the cooking of many cultures and is used in many different ways. Perhaps the best known is *baba ghanoush,* a Middle Eastern dip or spread in which hummus is added to the cooked eggplant.

The eggplant is a staple ingredient in many countries of the world, and it is known by many names. In Spain and Mexico, where it is called *berenjena,* eggplant is combined with ham, red bell peppers, garlic, mushrooms, and artichokes in a vegetable stew, *pisto,* and served hot or cold.

Italians combine *melanzana* with tomatoes to make pasta sauce and eggplant *parmigiana*. In Sicily, eggplants are the basis for the delicious antipasto, *capstan*.

Best known of all French eggplant dishes is *ratatouille Niçoise*, a stew of tomatoes, eggplant, onion, garlic, zucchini, peppers, and herbs.

A Rumanian method of preparing it is to bake the *vinete* until tender, then stuff with sautéed onions.

In Afghanistan, as in many Middle Eastern countries, the most popular way of serving it is in a dish called *buraunee baunjaun*, which is sautéed eggplant topped with a sauce of yogurt and garlic.

In Egypt, slices are often baked with a sweet tomato topping.

Greeks enjoy eggplant, or *melitzanes*, made into a sweet spicy preserve called *melitzanes glyko*, which is served as a condiment with roast meats. But Greeks enjoy it most of all in their famous *Moussaka*, layered with lamb and topped with cheese custard.

The Turkish dish, *imam bayildi* (literally "the fainting priest"), presumably got its name from the amount of olive oil used in the preparation. The Imam swooned in delight at the taste—or in dismay at the expense.

History

History is not the sole prerogative of humans. Plants also leave traces of their travels and migrations, they too are uprooted and re-established in new lands, they adapt to new cultures, and these movements are recorded throughout the centuries. Ernest Klein, an English etymologist, traced the Asian and European development of the eggplant's name from an ancient Indian word, *vatin-ganah*, which became *badin-gan* in Persian, then *al-badinjan* in Arabic, *alberginia* in Catalan and finally *aubergine* in French.

This etymological journey also traces the cultural journey of the eggplant, which, curiously enough, has never been discovered growing wild. In his *Vegetables of Ancient China*, Li-Hui-Lin states that there are references of eggplants growing in Chinese vegetable gardens around 500 BC. The Chinese first speculated on the possibility of eating eggplant *(ch'ieh)* in the 3rd century A.D. However, no one actually ate it until 300 years later.

Migrating from China, the eggplant family established new homes throughout the other countries of Asia, in all its different colors and shapes.

Europeans, however, were not to discover the culinary delights of the eggplant until comparatively late. No mention has been found in Greek or Roman writings, and it was not until the 17th century that clear reference is made to the eggplant's arrival from North Africa via Spain and Catalan. It was probably during that same period that it crossed over to North America.

Called *egg-apple* or *eggplant* when it was introduced to England during the Middle Ages, it was given the nickname *madman's apple*. It appears that solanine, which is found in large quantities in the small white variety, may cause a number of ailments, especially if the vegetable is eaten before it is ripe. During the 19th century, many botanists described the *Solanum oviserum* as a plant more suited to decoration than to nourishment.

Today, this fruit is best known in the southern regions of Europe, especially the long violet-colored variety, and Provence is by far its favorite home. During the Second World War it earned the nickname *souliers de Petain* ("Petain's shoes")—a striking example of its extraordinary ability to inspire linguistic flights of fancy.

Eggplant Varieties

In North America, the most common eggplant is the large cylindrical or pear-shape variety with a smooth, glossy, dark-purple skin. Known as the *Western* or *globe eggplant,* this includes varieties such as Black Beauty and Black Bell. Its flesh is cream-colored to green, its mild flavor spiced with a hint of bitterness. It has a soft texture that falls apart when cooked, making it a good foundation for dips and casseroles.

Other varieties are becoming more popular and easier to find. All can be used in the same way, with some allowance made for differences in size.

The *Italian* or *baby eggplant* looks like a miniature version of the Western variety, but has a more delicate skin and flesh. It is delicious steamed, sautéed, fried or combined with cantaloupe chunks on a skewer and grilled. The combination of nutty, smoky eggplant and musky, sweet melon is heavenly.

Japanese eggplant is a very narrow, straight eggplant ranging in color from solid purple to striated shades. It has tender, slightly sweet, nutty flesh and thin edible skin. It is good sautéed, stir-fried, deep-fried or grilled. When halved and grilled, its smoky flavor is unparalleled. This variety is also used for pickling.

Chinese eggplant is distinguished by its light, bright or neon-purple color. It has a thin, tender skin and is sweeter than most darker varieties. It is good for stir-frying, baking or halving and grilling.

Rosa Bianca, an Italian eggplant, is nearly round and has white skin with lavender streaks. Its white flesh has a sweet flavor and a creamy yet firm texture. It holds its shape when cooked and is a good all-purpose variety.

Lao Green Stripe, also called *Thai Green Stripe,* resembles a golf ball with a pointed "hat." Its striped skin is rather tough and its flesh is quite seedy with a strong flavor. It is especially good cut into chunks, simmered briefly and served crisp in curries.

Listada de Gandia is an Italian variety with a long oval shape and white and purple stripes. It has a slightly bitter skin and mild white flesh with a meaty, creamy texture. It holds its shape when cooked and is a good all-purpose variety.

Pintong Long comes from Taiwan and is a favorite for flavor. Long and slender, its skin ranges from deep purple to lavender, its "cap" from green to purple-black. Its white flesh has a sweet, nutty flavor and buttery texture. It is good in stir-fried dishes.

The *White Egg* eggplant looks like a chicken or duck egg. It is sweet, mild and a little watery-tasting, with fairly firm flesh that holds its shape when cooked; its skin is rather tough and usually not eaten. This variety is good for stuffing and grilling.

Thai Long Green has lime-green skin and velvety white flesh. It is long and slender and has a sweet, somewhat nutty flavor that has also been described as reminiscent of green beans. Most slices are seedless because the seed cavity is at the blossom end. It is good in stir-fried dishes.

Rosita, a Puerto Rican native, is bright lavender in color. It has a long oval shape, white flesh and a mild, sweet flavor. Its tender flesh and skin make it a good all-purpose eggplant.

Garden Egg is a variety of small, green-skinned African eggplant. The even smaller *pea eggplant* is a bitter southeast Asian variety that is best used in pickles. It can be purple, green, red or orange.

Growing Eggplant

Eggplant is a native of Asia but is widely grown in the warmer regions of both hemispheres, especially in the West Indies and southern United States. It is related to the tomato and responds to the same basic cultural care. Plants should be set in the garden in early spring after all danger of frost. Maintain the plants in a vigorous state of growth with adequate fertilizer and moisture.

Poor-quality eggplant fruit are generally associated with low moisture and high temperature conditions. Also, overmature eggplant fruit will become dull colored and often develop a bronze appearance. For maximum production, remove the eggplant fruit before they are fully mature to allow additional fruit to develop.

Small-fruited and ornamental varieties can be grown in containers or for decorative purposes.

Fruit should be large, shiny, and a uniformly deep-purple color. When the side of the fruit is pressed slightly with thumbnail and an indentation remains, the fruit is ripe. Long, slender Japanese eggplant may be ready to harvest at finger or hot-dog size. If fruit is a dull color and has brown seeds, it is too ripe—discard it.

The fruits of the eggplant are edible from the time they are one-third grown until ripe. They remain in an edible condition for several weeks after they become colored and fully grown. Skin should be shiny; seeds inside should not be brown or hard. Harvest will continue over an extended period if the fruit are removed when they are well-colored and of adequate size.

The fruits are usually cut from the plants because the stems are hard and woody. The large *calyx* (cap) and a short piece of stem are left on the fruit. Plants of most cultivars have sharp spines, so take care when harvesting to prevent injury.

Where to Order Eggplant Seed

Seeds Blüm
H.C. 33
Idaho City Stage
Boise, ID 83706
800-528-3658
($3 for catalog)

Southern Exposure Seed Exchange
Box 170
Earlysville, VA 22936
804-973-4703
($3 for catalog)

Stokes Seeds
Box 548
Buffalo, NY 14240
716-695-6980
(no charge for catalog)

Sunrise Enterprises
Box 1960
Chesterfield, VA 23832
804-796-5796
($2 for catalog)

Tips for Purchasing and Preparing Eggplant

First and foremost, it is best to choose eggplants that are fresh and firm, smooth and shiny. It is much better to delay preparing a dish than to buy vegetables that are obviously tired.

The best eggplants have fresh *calyxes* (caps of leaves surrounding stem) and smooth unbruised skin with a good sheen. Press gently on the skin. If it doesn't bounce back, but stays dented, it is not fresh. Very spongy eggplants have been on the shelf too long, while rock-hard ones were left on the plant too long. Another sign of over-maturity is color: Purple ones become bronze; white and green turn yellow. Choose eggplants that are heavy for their size; avoid those with soft or brown spots.

Look for male eggplants, which have fewer seeds (which are often bitter) than the female of the species; they have a rounder, smoother blossom end or base. The blossom end of a female egg-plant is generally indented.

Eggplants are very perishable. Store them in a cool, dry place and use within 1 to 2 days of purchase. If longer storage is necessary, place the eggplant in the refrigerator vegetable drawer, where they will keep for up to 5 days.

Eggplant is available all year, with the peak season from July to the end of September. Supermarkets carry mostly the familiar globe vari-eties. Asian stores will carry Asian varieties, although they may not be labeled as such. Farmers' markets usually offer the most variety.

Like its relative, the potato, the eggplant is extremely versatile. It can be baked, stewed, grilled, fried or boiled. It can be layered, shredded, chopped, diced, puréed or sliced. It can be stuffed, used as stuffing or wrapped around meat or cheese. And the resulting dishes can be anything from humble and homey to saucy and sophisticated.

Two pitfalls of cooking with eggplants are their bitterness and their propensity to absorb oil. There are techniques to deal with both of these problems.

Eggplants with dark-purple skin contain a bitter pigment *(antho-cyanin)* in the skin and just below it. The bitter taste disappears after about 20 minutes of cooking. If you are going to cook it less than that, lightly salt the cut vegetable, place it in a colander and let it stand for about 20 minutes. The salt will draw out the bitter juices. Wipe the eggplant carefully with a paper towel. There is no need to rinse it.

It is not necessary to salt eggplants that are small or that are going to be grilled. However, any variety will acquire a strong taste as seeds enlarge and get bitter, so avoid eggplants that are overripe.

Another way to eliminate bitterness is to peel the eggplant and to remove the layer of flesh closest to skin. Traditionally, eggplants that must be peeled are charred over an open fire. A gas flame or broiler also works well; when cool, the skin is easily removed.

It is true that eggplants absorb oil like a sponge, so avoid frying them if you're watching calories. There are several ways to reduce the amount of oil they will soak up:

1. Bake slices in a 325F (165C) oven for 25 minutes, or brush slices with oil and broil 5 minutes on each side, until golden.
2. Before grilling, lightly brush or spray slices with oil.
3. Before sautéing, place slices or cubes in a wok or skillet with a little water—1/4 cup (60ml) for 1 pound (450g) eggplant. Simmer, covered, until tender when pierced, about 5 minutes.
4. Before frying, batter slices, or dip in beaten egg, then bread crumbs. Let dry 30 minutes in the refrigerator before frying.
5. When brushing with oil, dip brush into oil and apply lightly to eggplant. *Never* pour oil directly onto eggplant—the oil will be absorbed before you can begin to spread it around.

Be sure to rinse eggplants and remove their stems, unless otherwise instructed. Young eggplants don't require peeling. If peeling is desired, a vegetable peeler works well, as does an ultra-sharp paring knife. Once peeled, the flesh discolors rapidly, so peel just before using. You can also brush the flesh with lemon juice or dip it in 1 quart cold water mixed with 3 tablespoons (45ml) lemon juice. One pound of eggplant will yield 3 to 4 cups chopped flesh.

To cook eggplant in the microwave, cut off the cap, remove the skin, if desired, and cut the flesh into 3/4-inch (2cm) cubes. Place them in a 2-quart (2-liter) casserole with 2 tablespoons (30ml) butter. Cover. Microwave on high 7 to 10 minutes. Stir every 2 minutes.

However you prepare eggplant, be sure it is thoroughly done. Only then does it become sweet and luscious. Even those who enjoy crisp vegetables will not welcome undercooked eggplant.

It is better not to use the electric mixer in recipes based on eggplants. The eggplant seeds, when chopped in the mixer, tend to give off a bitter taste which ruins the flavor. Using a food mill, on the other hand, leaves the seeds whole. In any event, if the eggplants have a lot of seeds, it is best to remove them before cooking.

Finally, all recipes specifying saucepans or casserole dishes can also be made in a pressure cooker. You should reduce the amount of liquid and expect the cooking time to be three times faster. However, nothing cooks better than a long slow simmer.

Many recipes call for tomatoes to be peeled and seeded. This is easily done by placing them in boiling water for 30 seconds and then in cold water. This loosens the skin so it slips right off. Cut the tomato in half and squeeze out the seeds.

Our way of living, especially in the city, unfortunately leaves us too little time to prepare dishes that require a number of tasks. The recipes which follow, being for the most part traditional dishes, do not take this factor into account. But this does not mean that some cannot be simplified without destroying the dish's flavor.

It is not absolutely necessary to make the eggplants sweat out their liquid. Even though this does provide three advantages (removes the naturally spicy taste, reduces the amount of oil absorbed and shortens the cooking time), there will be no major catastrophes if you decide to cook at the last moment and skip this step.

You can also gain time by using canned tomatoes in their juice or canned chopped tomatoes instead of fresh tomatoes. If you use either, do not forget to strain the juice before adding to the dish.

Special Ingredients

Brocciu

Corsican cheese.

Chile peppers

Chile peppers range in taste from mild to extremely hot. As a rule, milder chiles, such as the Anaheim, are longer and a lighter green than jalapeños and other hot chiles.

Dashi

Mild-flavored fish stock available in the Oriental section of most markets.

Eggplant caviar

A thick puréed mixture of roasted eggplant and other ingredients. It is used in a variety of ways, often as a dip or spread.

Garam masala

Mixture of ground spices used in Indian cooking: cinnamon, green cardamom, cloves, cumin, coriander and black pepper.

Mirin

A sweetened rice wine.

Myzithra

Mild, semi-hard Greek cheese.

Tahini

Thick paste made of ground sesame seed.

Tamarind

The fruit of the tamarind tree is popular in Indian cooking because of its sweet and acid taste. The pod resembles the pea and is 3 to 8 inches (8-20 cm) long. The fruit can be preserved in liquid or dried in the sun. Only the flesh is used in cooking. It is available both in its pod and in a packet with pressed flesh and crushed pod.

Cold Starters

*T*o get your meal off to an elegant start, turn to Eggplant Rolls with Avocado or Eggplant Fans. As delicious as they are beautiful, these appetizers will be sure to impress.

But starters don't have to be complicated to be good. Try Eggplant in Oregano Marinade or Greek-Style Fried Eggplant. Both are easy to make and tasty.

Offer your guests *Baba Ghanoush,* translated as "Eggplant Tahini Caviar," a staple in many countries of the Middle East. Or go Italian with *Caponata,* a traditional Sicilian side dish.

Most of these recipes can be served as side dishes, and many in this chapter and the next are good as luncheon entrées, too.

Eggplant Rolls with Avocado

Slice these rolls in two to reveal the colorful filling. Serve as a starter or luncheon entrée. To save time and effort, buy roasted bell peppers.

1 eggplant, about 1 lb. (450g)
Olive oil for frying
1/3 cup (80ml) ricotta cheese
1/3 cup (80ml) herbed feta cheese
2 tablespoons (30ml) chopped green olives
1 tablespoon (15ml) capers
3 green onions, chopped
1 avocado, peeled and sliced
1 tablespoon (15ml) lemon juice
3 red bell peppers, roasted and cut lengthwise into strips
Salt and pepper to taste
Sour cream for garnish

Preheat broiler. Lightly grease baking sheet. Cut eggplant lengthwise into 6 slices, discarding end pieces. Lightly brush or spray eggplant slices with oil and place on prepared baking sheet. Broil until golden, turn, brush or spray with oil and broil second side. Remove and place on paper towels to drain.

Combine cheeses, olives, capers and onions. In a separate dish, mash avocado and stir in lemon juice.

Place peppers in single layer on large end of eggplant slices. Season with salt and pepper. Spoon cheese mixture on narrow end of each slice. Carefully roll up and place, seam side down, on a serving dish. Garnish with dollops of sour cream and avocado. Serve cold or at room temperature.

Makes 6 servings.

Each serving contains:

Cal	Prot	Carb	Fib	Tot. Fat	Sat. Fat	Chol	Sodium
250	5g	11g	4g	22g	7g	21mg	344mg

Eggplant and Tomato Loaf

Pain d'Aubergines à la Tomate
(Provence)

Serve accompanied by a spicy tomato sauce or a tomato-mint sauce.

1 lb. (450g) eggplant, peeled
Salt
6 tablespoons (90ml) olive oil
Pepper
3 garlic cloves, crushed
3 onions, chopped
Herbes de Provence (thyme, rosemary, sage, oregano) to taste
4 eggs
1/4 cup (60ml) sour cream

Cut eggplant into 1-1/2-inch (4cm) cubes, sprinkle with salt and drain in colander 20 minutes. Pat dry with a paper towel.

Heat olive oil in a heavy skillet and sauté eggplant gently, stirring constantly. Raise heat and cook another 5 minutes. Season with salt and pepper and add garlic, onions and herbes de Provence. Mix well and simmer, uncovered, over low heat 30 minutes.

Heat oven to 425F (220C). Butter a loaf pan or mold. Beat eggs together with sour cream. When eggplant is cooked, mash with a fork. Add egg mixture and pour into prepared pan. Place in larger pan with at least 1 inch (2.5cm) hot water.

Cook in oven 30 minutes. Allow to cool, then refrigerate at least 3 hours.

Makes 6 servings.

Each serving contains:

Cal	Prot	Carb	Fib	Tot. Fat	Sat. Fat	Chol	Sodium
233	6g	11g	3g	19g	4g	146mg	96mg

Eggplant Fans
Aubergines en Eventail
(Provence)

If this dish is to be made the day before and kept in the refrigerator, take it out a few hours before serving. The oil congeals if left cold for too long, and this will affect the flavor.

> *7 tablespoons (105ml) olive oil*
> *2 onions, chopped*
> *1 lb. (450g) small eggplants*
> *3 tomatoes, cut into round slices*
> *Chopped parsley*
> *6 garlic cloves, crushed*
> *1 teaspoon (5ml) herbes de Provence (thyme, rosemary, sage,*
> *   oregano)*
> *Salt and pepper*
> *Black olives, capers, pine nuts or fresh basil leaves*

Heat oven to 400F (200C). Pour 2 tablespoons (30ml) olive oil into a baking dish and cover with onions.

Starting 1 inch (2.5cm) from the stem end of each eggplant, cut into slices lengthwise, from top to bottom. Fan out and arrange on top of onions.

Brush tomato slices with olive oil and sprinkle with parsley and garlic. Place between eggplant slices. Sprinkle with herbes de Provence, salt, pepper and olive oil. Cover with foil.

Bake in oven approximately 50 minutes. The eggplant should be almost melting! Remove foil and bake 10 minutes longer. Remove from oven and garnish with olives, capers, pine nuts or basil leaves.

Leave at room temperature until ready to serve.

Makes 6 servings.

Variations

1. Alternate zucchini slices with tomato slices.

2. Add an anchovy to each tomato slice.

3. Replace the onions with a mixture of onions and red peppers, which should be lightly cooked beforehand.

Each serving contains:

Cal	Prot	Carb	Fib	Tot. Fat	Sat. Fat	Chol	Sodium
205	2g	13g	4g	17g	2g	0mg	106mg

Basic Eggplant Caviar

The basic preparation method for eggplant caviar is used in many other recipes, and is referred to often in this cookbook.

To cook eggplant as for a caviar: Grill whole, unpeeled eggplants directly over flames, under a broiler or over a charcoal grill. They can also be cooked in a hot oven. Turn eggplants regularly, but do not remove from the heat until they are very soft. Carefully take hold of them by the stalk, to avoid being pricked. Peel and set aside in a colander to drain for 30 minutes. Mash or slice them, as directed in individual recipes.

Eggplant Caviar

Originally from Central Europe, eggplant caviar has found a home in every country where eggplants are grown. Each adds its local color and so there are many different ways of preparing and serving this dish. Serve it as a starter on slices of toasted rye or whole-grain bread decorated with slices of hard-cooked eggs. It can also be served on canapés to accompany drinks.

This recipe comes from the traditional Jewish cuisine of Bessarabia, an area located in the present Ukraine and Moldavia.

> *1 lb. (450g) eggplant*
> *2 onions, minced*
> *Sunflower oil*
> *Salt and pepper to taste*
> *Parsley to taste*
> *Lemon juice to taste*

Prepare eggplant according to basic caviar recipe, page 6. Mash eggplant flesh with a fork. Add onions and mix well. Add oil in a thin stream, mixing well to make a smooth paste. Add salt, pepper, parsley and lemon juice.

Serve while still warm or else very cold.

Makes 6 servings.

Variations
1. Replace onions with 3 crushed garlic cloves and use olive oil instead of sunflower oil. Add the juice of 1 lemon at the end.

2. Use mayonnaise instead of oil.

Each serving contains:

Cal	Prot	Carb	Fib	Tot. Fat	Sat. Fat	Chol	Sodium
119	1g	9g	3g	9g	1g	0mg	48mg

Eggplants Stuffed
with Onions and Tomatoes

Imam Bayeldi—Fainting Imam

(Armenia)

The Imam, or Muslim priest, swooned with delight when he tasted this dish. Try it for yourself.

> *6 small eggplants, total weight 1 lb. (450g)*
> *Salt*
> *4 tomatoes, peeled and chopped*
> *3 onions, thinly sliced*
> *12 large garlic cloves, halved (optional)*
> *Pepper to taste*
> *Olive oil for brushing*
> *1 tablespoon (15ml) sugar*

Peel eggplants, leaving a few bands of skin. Sprinkle with salt and drain in colander 20 minutes. Pat dry with paper towel. Combine tomatoes and onions.

Wipe eggplants with a cloth. Cut a slit down the side of each eggplant and fill with tomato-onion mixture and garlic halves, if using. Place in a large saucepan, brush with oil and sprinkle with sugar. Cover and cook over low heat 1 hour. Or bake uncovered in preheated 350F(175C) for 40 minutes. Serve cold.

Makes 6 servings.

Variation

Instead of tomatoes, onions and garlic, use the ground-lamb stuffing from Stuffed Eggplant Fans, page 134.

Each serving contains:

Cal	Prot	Carb	Fib	Tot. Fat	Sat. Fat	Chol	Sodium
116	2g	18g	4g	5g	1g	0mg	57mg

Eggplant Caviar with Black Olives

Caviar d'Aubergines aux Olives Noires
(Provence)

Who needs expensive beluga caviar when you can have this delicious version?

1 lb. (450g) eggplant
3 large garlic cloves, crushed
3/4 cup (185ml) pitted black olives, chopped
Salt and pepper to taste
Olive oil

Prepare eggplant according to basic caviar recipe, page 6. Mash with a fork. Add garlic, olives, salt and pepper. Mix well. Stirring constantly, pour in enough oil to make a smooth mixture. Serve cold.

Makes 6 servings.

Each serving contains:

Cal	Prot	Carb	Fib	Tot. Fat	Sat. Fat	Chol	Sodium
122	1g	7g	2g	10g	2g	0mg	191mg

Eggplant Tahini Caviar

Baba Ghanoush
(Lebanon)

Tahini is a paste made from ground sesame seeds and is an important ingredient in many Middle Eastern dishes.

1 lb. (450g) eggplant
3 garlic cloves, crushed
5 tablespoons (75ml) tahini
Juice of 1 lemon
1 tablespoon (15ml) chopped parsley
1 teaspoon (5ml) ground cumin
Salt and pepper to taste

Prepare eggplant according to basic caviar recipe, page 6. Mash with a fork. Add remaining ingredients. Mix well. Serve very cold.

Makes 6 servings.

Each serving contains:

Cal	Prot	Carb	Fib	Tot. Fat	Sat. Fat	Chol	Sodium
103	3g	9g	3g	7g	1g	0mg	48mg

Yogurt with Eggplant

Batigan Ka Raita

(India)

A *raita* is a cooked mixture of yogurt and vegetables or fruit, used also as a side dish or a relish. *Garam masala,* meaning "hot mixture of spices," comes in as many varieties as there are Indian cooks. You can make your own, or buy it ready-made.

> *1 lb. (450g) eggplant*
> *2 tablespoons (30ml) peanut or sunflower oil*
> *1 onion, finely chopped*
> *1 teaspoon (5ml) salt*
> *1 tomato, peeled and chopped*
> *4 teaspoons (20ml) chopped cilantro*
> *1 teaspoon (5ml) garam masala*
> *9 oz. (250g) yogurt*

Prepare eggplant according to basic caviar recipe, page 6. Mash eggplant flesh with a fork.

Heat oil in a heavy pan. Add onion and salt and simmer over low heat, stirring occasionally. When onion begins to turn golden, add tomato, cilantro and garam masala. Stir and cook a minute longer. Add eggplant, stir with a wooden spoon and cook 3 minutes. Set aside to cool.

In a large bowl, whisk yogurt; add eggplant mixture. Mix carefully and refrigerate 1 to 2 hours before serving.

Makes 6 servings.

Each serving contains:

Cal	Prot	Carb	Fib	Tot. Fat	Sat. Fat	Chol	Sodium
101	3g	10g	3g	6g	2g	5mg	381mg

Eggplant in Ginger Sauce

(Japan)

Rice vinegar is made from fermented rice and has a mild, somewhat sweet flavor. It is widely used in Japanese and Chinese cooking.

1 lb. (450g) eggplant, peeled
7 oz. (200g) fresh ginger, peeled
5 tablespoons (75ml) light soy sauce
2 tablespoons (30ml) rice vinegar or cider vinegar
2 teaspoons (10ml) sake (rice wine) (optional)
2 tablespoons (30ml) sesame seeds, roasted or dry-fried
1 onion, sliced

Cut eggplant lengthwise into 3/4-inch (2cm) slices. Steam over boiling water until tender. Or cook in pressure cooker 7 to 8 minutes. Set aside to cool.

Cut ginger into very thin slices. Combine soy sauce, vinegar and sake, if using. Cut eggplant slices into strips (2 x 1/2-inch / 5x1.25cm).

Spread eggplant in a deep dish; cover with ginger and then with sauce. Set aside to marinate for 3 hours, stirring occasionally.

Just before serving, sprinkle with sesame seeds and garnish with onion slices.

Makes 6 servings.

Each serving contains:

Cal	Prot	Carb	Fib	Tot. Fat	Sat. Fat	Chol	Sodium
79	3g	14g	3g	2g	0g	0mg	429mg

Eggplant in Oregano Marinade

(Sicily)

This simple dish gets any meal off to a good start.

Salt
1 lb. (450g) eggplant, peeled
2 tablespoons (30ml) olive oil
2 tablespoons (30ml) wine vinegar
1 tablespoon (15ml) dried oregano leaves
3 garlic cloves, crushed

Preheat broiler or heavy skillet. If using skillet, sprinkle it with salt.

Cut eggplant crosswise into 1/2-inch (1.25cm) slices and lay them on broiler rack or skillet. Cook 1 to 2 minutes on each side and remove to a shallow dish.

Combine oil, vinegar, oregano, garlic and a pinch of salt. Pour over eggplant. Set aside to marinate for at least 1 hour, stirring occasionally.

Makes 6 servings.

Each serving contains:

Cal	Prot	Carb	Fib	Tot. Fat	Sat. Fat	Chol	Sodium
66	1g	6g	2g	5g	1g	0mg	47mg

Savory Eggplant Dip
(Italy)

This unusual combination of flavors will bring you back for more.

1 lb. (450g) eggplant, peeled and diced
Peanut oil or sunflower oil for frying
Salt and pepper to taste
1/2 cup (125ml) chopped gherkin pickles
1/3 cup (80ml) capers, chopped
1-1/4 cups (310ml) pitted black olives, chopped

Cook eggplant gently in oil, first over high heat and then over medium heat, 5 to 10 minutes, until tender. Season with salt and pepper. Add remaining ingredients and cook gently 10 to 15 minutes, stirring occasionally. Set aside to cool.

Chill in refrigerator 1 to 2 hours before serving.

Makes 6 servings.

Each serving contains:

Cal	Prot	Carb	Fib	Tot. Fat	Sat. Fat	Chol	Sodium
107	1g	10g	3g	8g	1g	0mg	647mg

Caponata

(Sicily)

Caponata is a traditional Sicilian dish that can also be served as a side dish, a salad or a relish. Pine nuts and anchovies may also be added.

> *1 lb. 2 oz. (500g) eggplant*
> *1 lb. 2 oz. (500g) green bell peppers, diced*
> *1 onion, chopped*
> *Olive oil for frying*
> *3 tomatoes, peeled and chopped*
> *1/4 cup (60ml) capers*
> *1/2 cup (125ml) pitted green olives*
> *1 large celery rib, chopped*
> *Salt to taste*
> *1/2 cup (125ml) wine vinegar*
> *1/2 cup (125ml) water*
> *1 teaspoon (5ml) sugar*

Without peeling, chop eggplant into small dice. Cook eggplant, peppers and onion in olive oil over low heat until soft.

Add tomatoes, capers, olives and celery and cook 5 to 10 minutes over low heat, stirring carefully, until all ingredients are cooked. Season with salt. Remove from heat.

Combine vinegar and water and pour over vegetables. Sprinkle with sugar and stir thoroughly. Pour into a serving dish and refrigerate 6 to 8 hours.

Makes 6 servings.

Variation
Serve hot over fettuccine.

Each serving contains:

Cal	Prot	Carb	Fib	Tot. Fat	Sat. Fat	Chol	Sodium
172	3g	20g	5g	11g	1g	0mg	500mg

Spicy Eggplants with Salsa

The small White Egg variety is probably the origin of the name *egg-plant*. It reached England sometime during the Middle Ages, when it was also known as *egg-apple* and *laying hen*.

> *20 White Egg eggplants (3-4 inches / 7-10cm)*
> *Oil for frying*
> *Salt to taste*
> *Ground cumin to taste*
> *3 garlic cloves, finely chopped*
> *Fresh Tomato Salsa, below*

Peel eggplants and cut lengthwise into thin slices. Heat a little oil in a skillet and fry eggplant slices. Drain on paper towels. Season with salt and sprinkle with cumin and garlic. Top with salsa and serve.

Makes 6 servings.

Each serving contains:

Cal	Prot	Carb	Fib	Tot. Fat	Sat. Fat	Chol	Sodium
118	1g	9g	3g	9g	1g	0mg	53mg

Fresh Tomato Salsa

1 chile pepper, roasted, peeled and chopped
2 fresh tomatoes, seeded and chopped
2 green onions, chopped
1 tablespoon (15ml) chopped cilantro or parsley
1 tablespoon (15ml) lemon juice

Combine all ingredients.

Makes 1 to 1-1/2 cups (250-375ml).

One serving contains:

Cal	Prot	Carb	Fib	Tot. Fat	Sat. Fat	Chol	Sodium
14	1g	3g	1g	0g	0g	0mg	5mg

Eggplants Stuffed with Peppers and Tomatoes

This beautiful fruit begs to be stuffed, and this colorful mixture is just one of many ways to do it.

3 eggplants, halved, total weight 1 lb. (450g)
3 tablespoons (45ml) olive oil
1 onion, minced
1 green bell pepper, cut into thin slices
1 red bell pepper, cut into thin slices
1 large garlic clove, minced
Salt and pepper to taste
Pinch of oregano
3 tomatoes, peeled and chopped
Juice of 1 lemon
3 tablespoons (45ml) chopped parsley
2 tablespoons (30ml) chopped cilantro
Mint leaves for garnish

Place eggplant halves, skin side up, in a steamer and cook 5 minutes. Carefully remove the flesh with a spoon, leaving a 1/4-inch (6mm) layer next to skin. Leave skin intact. Chop the flesh.

Heat 2 tablespoons (30ml) olive oil in large skillet. Cook chopped eggplant, onions, peppers and garlic, stirring constantly. Season with salt and pepper. Continue to cook uncovered over low heat 20 minutes, stirring occasionally. Add oregano and set aside to cool.

When very cool, add tomatoes, remaining oil, lemon juice, parsley and cilantro. Mix thoroughly. Fill eggplant skins with this mixture, garnish with mint leaves and refrigerate 2 hours.

Makes 6 servings.

Each serving contains:

Cal	Prot	Carb	Fib	Tot. Fat	Sat. Fat	Chol	Sodium
118	2g	14g	4g	7g	1g	0mg	57mg

Eggplants with Feta

Melitzanes Me Lathi

(Greece)

Flavored feta cheese is a wonderful addition to many dishes. Look for it in your favorite supermarket.

> *6 long eggplants, total weight 1 lb. (450g)*
> *Olive oil for frying*
> *2-1/4 lb. (1kg) ripe tomatoes, peeled*
> *1 onion, finely chopped*
> *6 garlic cloves, crushed*
> *1/2 cup (125ml) chopped parsley*
> *Salt and pepper to taste*
> *1 tablespoon (15ml) sugar*
> *1/2 cup (125ml) crumbled feta cheese with herbs or sun-dried tomatoes*

Cut off stem end of each eggplant and make a deep cut lengthwise. Heat oil in a skillet and sauté eggplants over low heat 10 minutes, turning them occasionally. Remove and set aside.

Chop 2 tomatoes and set the rest aside. Add chopped tomatoes, onion, garlic and parsley to skillet. Season with salt and pepper. Cook 15 minutes over low heat.

Preheat oven to 325F (160C). Stuff eggplants with tomato mixture and place in a baking dish. Push remaining tomatoes through a sieve and pour over eggplants. Sprinkle with salt, pepper and sugar.

Cover and bake 45 to 60 minutes. Serve cold, sprinkled with cheese.

Makes 6 servings.

Each serving contains:

Cal	Prot	Carb	Fib	Tot. Fat	Sat. Fat	Chol	Sodium
147	4g	19g	4g	7g	2g	8mg	169mg

Greek-Style Fried Eggplant
Melitzanes Tighanties

These slices can be served just as they are, dusted with parsley and garlic, or topped with a tomato sauce.

1 lb. (450g) small eggplants, cut into thin round slices
Salt
Flour for coating
Olive oil for frying
Pepper to taste
Chopped parsley to taste
Chopped garlic cloves to taste
1 recipe Tomato Sauce, page 119

Sprinkle eggplant rounds with salt and drain in colander 20 minutes. Dip slices in flour.

Heat oil in a skillet and sauté eggplant. Drain on paper towels. Place in serving dish. Sprinkle with salt, pepper, parsley and garlic and top with tomato sauce. Serve cold.

Makes 6 servings.

Variation
Make a batter (Eggplant Monte Cristo, page 26). Dip slices in batter before frying. Serve hot or cold.

Each serving contains:

Cal	Prot	Carb	Fib	Tot. Fat	Sat. Fat	Chol	Sodium
187	3g	20g	4g	12g	2g	0mg	324mg

Hot Starters

*T*hroughout the Middle East, the appetizer course is known as the *meze table,* and it is a cultural event. Lebanese and Turkish meze tables may offer as many as 40 hot and cold dishes, sometimes all at once, sometimes one at a time. In other places the table is less elaborate, but everywhere the purpose is socializing—singing, storytelling, discussing or just relaxing.

You might not want to prepare a meze table of just eggplant dishes—but you could, with the variety in this chapter. Some you can eat with your fingers— Hot Eggplant-Cheese Appetizers and Eggplant Monte Cristo, for example. Others, such as Eggplant in Chile Sauce and Eggplant in White Wine, might be scooped up in a slice of bread, as is done in that part of the world.

Add four kinds of stuffed eggplants, two tart recipes, and Eggplant Bruschetta, and there is enough variety to satisfy everyone.

Eggplant in Chile Sauce

(Middle East)

Capsaicin, the compound that gives chile peppers their heat, can also irritate your skin and eyes. Be sure to wash your hands and chopping utensils thoroughly after working with chiles. Most of the capsaicin is found in the seeds and membranes of the pepper, so remove them unless you want a very hot dish.

> *1 lb. (450g) eggplant*
> *Salt*
> *Oil for frying*
> *Chile Sauce, below*
> *Yogurt Sauce, below*
> *3 tablespoons (45ml) chopped fresh mint or cilantro*

Remove stems from eggplant and peel off strips of skin, leaving bands of black and white. Cut into cubes, sprinkle with salt and drain in colander 20 minutes. Pat dry with a paper towel.

Heat oil in skillet and cook eggplant until golden. Drain on paper towels.

Place in warm dish and cover with warm chile sauce. Pour yogurt sauce on top. Garnish with mint or cilantro. Serve hot.

Makes 6 servings.

Each serving contains:

Cal	Prot	Carb	Fib	Tot. Fat	Sat. Fat	Chol	Sodium
183	3g	12g	3g	15g	5g	16mg	179mg

Chile Sauce

2 tablespoons (30ml) butter or oil
4 tomatoes, peeled, seeded and chopped
1 tablespoon (15ml) tomato paste
1 green chile pepper, chopped
Salt to taste

Heat butter or oil in skillet, add tomatoes, tomato paste and chile pepper. Season with salt and add a little water. Cook gently, stirring occasionally, until sauce is desired consistency. Keep warm.

Makes 2-1/2 cups (625ml).

One serving contains:

Cal	Prot	Carb	Fib	Tot. Fat	Sat. Fat	Chol	Sodium
68	1g	6g	1g	5g	3g	12mg	136mg

Yogurt Sauce

1 cup (225g) yogurt
1 garlic clove, crushed

Combine yogurt and garlic. Keep cool.

Makes 1 cup (250ml).

One serving contains:

Cal	Prot	Carb	Fib	Tot. Fat	Sat. Fat	Chol	Sodium
26	1g	2g	0g	1g	1g	5mg	19mg

23

Hot Eggplant-Cheese Appetizers
Patlicab Köftesi
(Turkey)

Be sure to make plenty of these delicacies. They will disappear quickly.

1 lb. (450g) eggplant, peeled and cubed
2 cups (500ml) water
Juice of 1 lemon
3 tablespoons (45ml) butter
4 tablespoons (60ml) flour
1/2 cup (125ml) milk
3/4-1 cup (185-250ml) grated Romano or pecorino cheese
  (3-4 oz. / 85-115g)
1 teaspoon (5ml) salt
1 tablespoon (15ml) chopped parsley
Oil for frying
3 eggs, beaten
Lemon slices for garnish
Fresh mint leaves for garnish

Parboil eggplant cubes 5 to 7 minutes. Drain and place in a bowl containing water and lemon juice and set aside to marinate.

Melt butter in a saucepan. Stir in half the flour and blend well. Stir in milk a little at a time. Cook and stir 2 minutes and then add cheese, salt and parsley. Mix carefully and quickly. Remove from heat.

Drain eggplant and press to remove excess liquid. Add to cheese mixture and whisk together until well combined. Chill in refrigerator 2 hours.

Heat oil in a deep skillet. Form small amounts of cold purée into balls, roll in remaining flour and dip into eggs. Cook in hot oil. Remove with a slotted spoon and drain on paper towels.

Serve hot, garnished with lemon slices and mint leaves.

Makes 6 servings.

Each serving contains:

Cal	Prot	Carb	Fib	Tot. Fat	Sat. Fat	Chol	Sodium
286	10g	12g	2g	23g	9g	141mg	661mg

Eggplant Monte Cristo

(Turkey)

Try these sandwiches-with-a-difference as a snack or add a bowl of soup and turn them into lunch.

1 lb. (450g) long, thin eggplants, peeled
Salt
1 cup (250ml) flour
2 eggs
1 tablespoon (15ml) oil
Warm water
9 oz. (250g) feta cheese
3 tablespoons (45ml) capers, drained
1/4 teaspoon (1ml) garlic powder
Oil for frying
Sliced pimento-stuffed olives for garnish

Cut eggplants crosswise into 1/2-inch (1.25cm) slices. Sprinkle with salt and drain in colander 20 minutes. Pat dry with a paper towel.

Combine flour, eggs, oil and enough warm water to make a thick batter. Combine cheese, capers and garlic powder. Heat oil.

Make a sandwich with a thin layer of cheese mixture between two slices of eggplant, press together and spear with a fork. Dip into batter. Cook 3 to 4 minutes in very hot oil. Place on paper towels to drain. Repeat for remaining ingredients. Cut in half before serving. Garnish with olives. Serve hot.

Makes 6 servings.

Each serving contains:

Cal	Prot	Carb	Fib	Tot. Fat	Sat. Fat	Chol	Sodium
347	13g	23g	3g	23g	9g	109mg	779mg

Cheddar Soufflé

Eggplants, small or large, lend themselves beautifully to being stuffed.

6 small eggplants, total weight 1 lb. (450g)
Onion Sauce, below
1 garlic clove, crushed
2 eggs, separated
1/2 cup (125ml) grated Cheddar cheese (2 oz. / 60g)
1 teaspoon (5ml) dried tarragon
Salt and pepper to taste

Preheat oven to 400F (200C). Cut eggplants in half lengthwise. Bake, cut side up, until very soft. Remove from oven and reduce oven temperature to 350F (180C). Grease a baking dish large enough to hold eggplant halves in a single layer.

Remove flesh from eggplants with a spoon, leaving a 1/4-inch (6mm) layer next to skin. Place skins in prepared baking dish.

Mash eggplant flesh and add to onion sauce. Add garlic, egg yolks, half the cheese, tarragon, salt and pepper, stirring carefully until the mixture is well blended. Beat egg whites until stiff and carefully fold into mixture.

Fill eggplant skins with soufflé and sprinkle with remaining cheese. Return to oven and bake 15 minutes. Serve immediately.

Makes 6 servings.

Each serving contains:

Cal	Prot	Carb	Fib	Tot. Fat	Sat. Fat	Chol	Sodium
139	7g	11g	2g	7g	5g	88mg	166mg

Onion Sauce

1 tablespoon (15ml) butter
1 onion, finely chopped
2 tablespoons (30ml) flour
1 cup (250ml) milk

Melt butter and cook onion over low heat. Sprinkle in flour, stirring constantly. Pour milk in all at once and cook gently, stirring constantly, until sauce is thick. Remove from heat.

Makes 1 to 1-1/2 cups (250-375ml) sauce.

One serving contains:

Cal	Prot	Carb	Fib	Tot. Fat	Sat. Fat	Chol	Sodium
57	2g	5g	0g	3g	2g	10mg	40mg

Eggplants with Gruyère and Ricotta

(Greece)

Make sure the cooking oil is hot enough to sear the cut side of the eggplants and seal in the filling.

> *6 small eggplants, total weight 1 lb. (450g)*
> *Salt*
> *10 oz. (280g) ricotta cheese*
> *2 eggs*
> *Pepper to taste*
> *1/2 cup (125ml) finely grated Gruyère cheese (2 oz. / 60g)*
> *1/4 cup (60ml) chopped pimento*
> *1 teaspoon (5ml) dried oregano*
> *Flour*
> *Olive oil or peanut oil for frying*

Cut eggplants in half lengthwise. Remove flesh with a spoon, leaving a 1/4-inch (6mm) layer next to skin. Sprinkle skins and flesh with salt and drain in separate colanders for 20 minutes. Pat dry with paper towels. Finely chop flesh.

Combine ricotta and eggs and add to eggplant flesh. Season with salt and pepper and add cheese, pimento and oregano. Fill eggplant skins with mixture and sprinkle with flour. Heat oil in a skillet and cook eggplants, beginning filled side down. Turn several times while cooking. Serve immediately.

Makes 6 servings.

Each serving contains:

Cal	Prot	Carb	Fib	Tot. Fat	Sat. Fat	Chol	Sodium
253	11g	8g	2g	20g	7g	105mg	140mg

Eggplants with Sun-Dried Tomatoes

(Italy)

If you have dry-packed sun-dried tomatoes, soften in hot water for 10 minutes before chopping.

Peanut oil
3 round eggplants, total weight 1 lb. (450g)
10 oz. (280g) fresh ricotta cheese
1/4 lb. (115g) pancetta or lean bacon, diced
6 sun-dried tomato halves, chopped and drained
Salt and pepper to taste
Ground nutmeg to taste
Ground cinnamon to taste
3 tablespoons (45ml) breadcrumbs
6 tablespoons (90ml) grated Parmesan cheese (1-1/2 oz. / 45g)
3 egg yolks
1 tablespoon (15ml) chopped parsley

Preheat oven to 425F (220C). Grease baking dish with peanut oil.

Cut eggplants in half lengthwise. Remove flesh with a spoon, leaving a 1/4-inch (6mm) layer next to skin. Cook skins in a steamer for 10 minutes, then place in prepared baking dish and season lightly with salt. Steam eggplant flesh for 5 minutes and mash with a fork.

Combine ricotta, pancetta or bacon, sun-dried tomatoes, salt, pepper, nutmeg, cinnamon, 1 tablespoon (15ml) breadcrumbs and 4 tablespoons (60ml) grated cheese. Add egg yolks, parsley and eggplant flesh, stirring constantly. Fill eggplant halves with mixture. Combine remaining cheese and breadcrumbs and sprinkle over fillings. Bake 1 hour. Serve hot.

Makes 6 servings.

Each serving contains:

Cal	Prot	Carb	Fib	Tot. Fat	Sat. Fat	Chol	Sodium
262	13g	12g	3g	19g	8g	140mg	427mg

Blue Cheese and Eggplant Mousse

Papetoun de Merinjano
(Provence)

This is also nice cooked in individual dishes. Reduce the baking time
to 15 to 20 minutes and place under a broiler until the cheese melts.

2 tablespoons (30ml) butter
1 lb. (450g) eggplant, peeled
Salt
Olive oil for frying
2 eggs, beaten
3 tablespoons (45ml) milk
Pepper
Grated nutmeg
3/4 cup (185ml) crumbled blue cheese
1 teaspoon (5ml) dried tarragon

Preheat oven to 425F (220C). Grease a soufflé dish with butter. Cut
eggplant crosswise into 1/2-inch (1.25cm) slices. Sprinkle with salt
and drain in colander 20 minutes. Pat dry with a a paper towel.

Sauté eggplant slices in hot olive oil, then drain on paper towels. Push
eggplant through a food mill or purée in food processor. Add eggs,
milk, salt, pepper and a little nutmeg and mix carefully. Pour into
prepared soufflé dish and bake 30 minutes.

Preheat broiler. Combine blue cheese and tarragon. Sprinkle over
eggplant mousse and place under broiler about 10 minutes. Serve
hot.

Makes 6 servings.

Each serving contains:

Cal	Prot	Carb	Fib	Tot. Fat	Sat. Fat	Chol	Sodium
223	7g	6g	2g	20g	7g	95mg	346mg

Eggplant Tartlets
Tartelettes aux Aubergines
(Provence)

Eggplants are used abundantly in European cooking and combine beautifully with other late-summer produce, such as tomatoes, onions and peppers.

Pastry:
2 cups (500ml) flour
Pinch of salt
2/3 cup (160ml) butter, cut into small pieces
1 tablespoon (15ml) oil
5-7 tablespoons (75-105ml) cold water

Filling:
1 onion, chopped
1 tablespoon (15ml) olive oil
2 garlic cloves, crushed
1 red bell pepper, chopped
7 oz. (200g) eggplant, peeled and cubed
4 ripe tomatoes, peeled and chopped
1 tablespoon (15ml) chopped basil
Salt and pepper to taste
1 egg, beaten
7 tablespoons (105ml) sour cream
1/2 cup (125ml) grated Gruyère cheese (2 oz. / 60g) (optional)

Make pastry: Combine flour, salt and butter, working quickly with fingertips or pastry blender. Add oil and blend. Add water gradually, stirring constantly until dough is smooth and elastic. Shape into a ball and refrigerate for at least 1 hour.

Preheat oven to 400F (200C). Grease small individual tart molds. Roll out and cut pastry to fit molds. Prick pastry with a fork and cover with foil. Weight down with dried beans. Bake 10 minutes. Remove beans and foil.

Make filling: Sauté onion in hot oil. Add garlic, bell pepper, eggplant, tomatoes, basil, salt and pepper. Simmer over low heat about 15 minutes. Fill tartlets with the mixture.

Cover each tartlet with a little beaten egg, some sour cream and grated cheese, if using. Return to oven and bake 20 minutes. Serve warm.

Makes 6 servings.

Each serving contains:

Cal	Prot	Carb	Fib	Tot. Fat	Sat. Fat	Chol	Sodium
461	8g	42g	4g	30g	16g	98mg	328mg

Eggplant Parcels with Tomato and Basil

(United States)

There is no need to peel the garlic bulb; just trim off the top. After cooking, push out the individual cloves for garnish.

4 eggplants, total weight 1 lb. (450g)
Salt and pepper to taste
14 oz. (400g) tomatoes
2 roasted green chile peppers, peeled and sliced
3/4-1 cup (185-250ml) butter, cut into pieces
1 whole garlic bulb (10-12 cloves)
3 cups (750ml) water
Chopped basil to taste

Cut ends from eggplants. Make 2 long slits in one side of each, about three-quarters deep. Season with salt and pepper, drain in colander for 20 minutes. Pat dry with paper towels.

Cut tomatoes in half and then into 1/2-inch (1.25cm) slices. Stuff slits in eggplants with half-circles of tomato and slices of chile pepper. Place in Dutch oven or heavy skillet, add butter, the whole garlic bulb, water and 1/2 to 1 teaspoon (2-5ml) salt. Cover and cook over low heat 30 minutes.

Remove eggplants. Set aside and keep warm. Simmer cooking liquid until it becomes syrupy.

Transfer eggplants to serving dish, cover with pan juices and sprinkle with basil. Carefully separate garlic cloves and use as garnish. Serve very hot.

Makes 4 servings.

Cold variation
Replace butter with I cup (250ml) olive oil plus juice of half a lemon. Reduce pan juices further and then place in refrigerator in a separate dish. Serve eggplants and juice at room temperature.

Each serving contains:

Cal	Prot	Carb	Fib	Tot. Fat	Sat. Fat	Chol	Sodium
478	3g	16g	4g	47g	29g	124mg	889mg

Eggplant Tart Provençal

Tarte aux Aubergines

Eggplant, olives and onions are three ingredients that mark a dish as being from Provence, a region in southeastern France.

Pastry:
2 cups (500ml) flour
Pinch of salt
2/3 cup (160ml) butter, cut into small pieces
1 egg
6-8 tablespoons (90-125ml) water

Filling:
2-1/4 lb. (1kg) eggplant, peeled and sliced crosswise
Oil for frying
Salt and pepper
5 oz. (145g) ricotta cheese (2/3 cup / 160ml)
1 egg, beaten
3 green onions, chopped
2 tablespoons (30ml) chopped fresh parsley
2 tablespoons (30ml) sliced green olives

Make pastry: Combine flour, salt, butter and egg, working quickly with fingertips. Add water gradually, stirring constantly until dough is smooth and elastic. Shape into a ball and refrigerate 30 to 60 minutes.

Preheat oven to 375F (190C). Grease a tart pan. Roll out pastry and line prepared pan. Prick crust all over with a fork and cover with foil. Weight down with dried beans. Bake 15 minutes. Remove beans and foil. Increase oven temperature to 400F (200C).

Make filling: Cook eggplant slices gently in oil. Drain and cool on paper towels. Season with salt and pepper. Mix cheese and egg together thoroughly; season with salt and pepper. Add eggplant, green onions, parsley and olives.

Pour eggplant mixture into cooked pastry, and bake 20 minutes. Serve warm.

Makes 6 servings.

Each serving contains:

Cal	Prot	Carb	Fib	Tot. Fat	Sat. Fat	Chol	Sodium
526	11g	44g	6g	35g	17g	138mg	393mg

Eggplant in White Wine

Confit d'Aubergines
(Provence)

Vary the amounts of herbs according to your own taste. Remember that the flavor of herbs intensifies when they are dried.

1 lb. (450g) eggplant
6 tablespoons (90ml) olive oil
3 oz. (85g) salt pork, diced
1 large onion, sliced
3 garlic cloves, crushed
Salt and pepper to taste
Thyme to taste
Summer savory to taste
Rosemary to taste
Bay leaves to taste
4 tomatoes, peeled and chopped
1 cup (250ml) dry white wine
1 tablespoon (15ml) chopped parsley
2 tablespoons (30ml) breadcrumbs (optional)

Cut eggplant crosswise into thick slices, without peeling. Pour oil into a saucepan. Add salt pork, onions, garlic, salt, pepper and all herbs except parsley. Add tomatoes and eggplant.

Place over high heat until mixture begins to boil, then reduce heat to low. Allow juices to reduce in volume. Cover and simmer about 30 minutes.

Spread eggplant carefully in the dish and add wine and parsley. Add breadcrumbs if you want a thicker sauce. Simmer 30 minutes longer, discard bay leaf and serve.

Makes 6 servings.

Each serving contains:

Cal	Prot	Carb	Fib	Tot. Fat	Sat. Fat	Chol	Sodium
268	2g	13g	4g	21g	5g	7mg	99mg

Sautéed Eggplant Topped with Tomatoes

(Tunisia)

This North African appetizer also makes a delicious side dish.

1 lb. (450g) eggplant, sliced lengthwise
Salt
6 tomatoes, halved and seeded
Cooking oil
1 tablespoon (15ml) chopped parsley
3 garlic cloves, crushed
Salt and pepper
Wine vinegar

Sprinkle eggplant slices with salt and drain 20 minutes in colander. Pat dry with a paper towel.

In a large pan, sauté tomatoes in oil, turning frequently. Remove from pan and keep warm. Sauté eggplant slices in same pan; drain on paper towels.

Arrange eggplant slices in a heated serving dish, cover with tomato halves and sprinkle with parsley, garlic, salt and pepper. Top with a little vinegar. Serve warm.

Makes 6 servings.

Each serving contains:

Cal	Prot	Carb	Fib	Tot. Fat	Sat. Fat	Chol	Sodium
130	2g	11g	3g	10g	1g	0mg	58mg

Eggplant Bruschetta

Small Japanese eggplants are the ideal size for this toasted appetizer.
Use the long narrow French bread called a *baguette*.

> *1 small eggplant, 1/2 lb. (225g)*
> *2-3 tablespoons (30-45ml) olive oil plus oil for brushing*
> *1/4 teaspoon (1ml) minced garlic*
> *1 teaspoon (5ml) chopped fresh parsley*
> *1 loaf French bread, cut into 12 slices*
> *12 thin slices ham*
> *2-3 fresh tomatoes, sliced*
> *Shredded mozzarella cheese*
> *Chopped black olives*

Cut eggplant into 6 crosswise slices, 1/4 inch (6mm) thick. Brush or
spray both sides with oil and broil or grill until tender. Remove and
drain on paper towels.

Mix 2 to 3 tablespoons (30-45ml) oil with garlic and parsley. Place
bread on baking sheet. Brush one side of each bread slice with oil
mixture. Broil or bake bread until lightly toasted.

Top bread slices with ham, tomatoes and cheese. Sprinkle with olives.
Return to broiler or oven and heat until cheese softens. Serve warm.

Makes 6 servings.

Each serving contains:

Cal	Prot	Carb	Fib	Tot. Fat	Sat. Fat	Chol	Sodium
182	13g	10g	2g	11g	3g	30mg	909mg

Salads

The eight salads in this chapter show off many uses of eggplant, from the traditional Greek *Melitzanosalata* to Eggplant Terrine from Algeria. For a change of pace, for your next party prepare Eggplant Aspic. The colorful Tri-Pepper Salad is a contrast of textures and flavors, the sweetness of peppers and pine nuts and the sharpness of onions and olives.

An ideal summer salad, Eggplant Salad with Walnut Dressing provides a colorful, light combination. Crunchy walnuts give added texture.

Combine golden eggplant cubes with tomatoes, sliced onions and herbs to make Aromatic Eggplant Salad, or use leftover ham in Tangy Eggplant-Ham Salad.

Eggplant Aspic

(England)

A refreshing salad that highlights the subtle flavor of the eggplant, with interest added by the greens and garnishes.

1 lb. (450g) eggplant
2 tablespoons (30ml) olive oil
Juice of 1 lemon
Salt and pepper to taste
2 tablespoons (30ml) unflavored gelatin (2 packets)
1 cup (250ml) cold water
Salad greens to taste
Lemon slices to taste
Cucumber slices to taste
Black olives to taste
A few sprigs of fresh mint

Prepare eggplant according to basic caviar recipe, page 6. Mash with a fork. Add oil slowly, stirring constantly. Add lemon juice, salt and pepper.

Sprinkle gelatin into cold water and soften for 3 to 5 minutes. Add to eggplant and mix thoroughly. Rinse 6 small dishes or a 6-cup (1.5-liter) mold in cold water, and, without drying, pour in eggplant mixture. Refrigerate 6 to 8 hours.

Place greens on individual plates or serving plate. Turn aspic onto greens. Garnish with lemon slices, cucumber slices, olives and mint.

Makes 6 servings.

Variations
1. Soften gelatin in wine vinegar.

2. Add 2/3 cup (160ml) tomato juice and 8 oz. (225g) beaten yogurt.

Each serving contains:

Cal	Prot	Carb	Fib	Tot. Fat	Sat. Fat	Chol	Sodium
79	4g	7g	3g	5g	1g	0mg	78mg

Aromatic Eggplant Salad

Serve this salad heaped into lettuce-leaf boats.

1 lb. (450g) eggplant, peeled
Salt
1/4 cup (60ml) olive oil
1 large onion, finely chopped
2 large garlic cloves, crushed
4 ripe tomatoes, peeled, seeded and chopped
Chopped parsley to taste
Chopped basil or mint to taste
Juice of 1/2 lemon
Pepper to taste

Cut eggplant into 1/2-inch (1.25cm) cubes, sprinkle with salt and drain in colander 20 minutes. Pat dry with a paper towel.

Heat oil in a heavy-based pan and cook onion and eggplant until golden. Reduce heat to low and cook 10 to 15 minutes, stirring often. Add garlic and tomato and cook 2 to 3 minutes.

Place in serving dish and set aside to cool. Remove any excess oil. Add herbs and lemon juice. Season with salt and pepper.

Makes 4 to 6 servings.

Each serving contains:

Cal	Prot	Carb	Fib	Tot. Fat	Sat. Fat	Chol	Sodium
194	3g	17g	5g	14g	2g	0mg	83mg

Tri-Pepper Salad

(Armenia)

This salad goes particularly well with meat kebabs. Take advantage of the barbecue to grill the eggplant and other vegetables, as the tang of wood smoke will make them even tastier.

1 lb. (450g) eggplant
1 green bell pepper
1 red bell pepper
1 yellow bell pepper
3 tomatoes, peeled and chopped
1 onion, chopped, or 2 garlic cloves, crushed
2 tablespoons (30ml) pine nuts
2 tablespoons (30ml) green olives
Salt and pepper
1 tablespoon (15ml) olive oil
Juice of 1 lemon
Chopped parsley to taste

Prepare eggplant according to basic caviar recipe, page 6. Chop into small pieces.

Grill peppers, peel them, remove seeds and slice thinly. Add eggplant, tomatoes, onion or garlic, pine nuts and olives. Season with salt and pepper.

Combine oil and lemon juice. Pour over vegetables and sprinkle with parsley. Serve cold.

Makes 6 servings.

Each serving contains:

Cal	Prot	Carb	Fib	Tot. Fat	Sat. Fat	Chol	Sodium
98	3g	13g	4g	5g	1g	0mg	86mg

Eggplant Caviar Salad

Melitzanosalata

(Greece)

This traditional Greek salad also makes a good starter. Cooking the eggplant over a wood fire imparts a wonderful, smoky flavor.

1 lb. (450g) eggplant
1 large tomato, peeled and chopped
1 onion, chopped
2 garlic cloves, crushed
1/4 cup (60ml) olive oil
1 tablespoon (15ml) vinegar or lemon juice
Salt and pepper to taste
12 black olives
2 green bell peppers, cut into rings

Prepare eggplant according to basic caviar recipe, page 6. Mash with a fork. Add tomato, onion and garlic. Add oil, stirring constantly. Add vinegar or lemon juice. Season with salt and pepper. Serve cold, garnished with olives and pepper rings.

Makes 6 servings.

Each serving contains:

Cal	Prot	Carb	Fib	Tot. Fat	Sat. Fat	Chol	Sodium
132	1g	10g	3g	10g	1g	0mg	129mg

Eggplant Salad with Walnut Dressing

(Georgia, Armenia)

Grenadine is a deep-red syrup made from pomegranates. It will make a sweeter dressing than the wine vinegar.

> *1 lb. (450g) eggplant, cut lengthwise into 1/2-inch (1.25cm) slices.*
> *Salt*
> *1/4 cup (60ml) sunflower oil*
> *1-1/2 cups (375ml) shelled walnuts, chopped*
> *2 garlic cloves, chopped*
> *Bunch of cilantro, chopped*
> *1 teaspoon (5ml) sugar*
> *Freshly ground pepper*
> *2 tablespoons (30ml) wine vinegar or grenadine juice*
> *1 cup (250ml) cold water*
> *Lettuce*

Sprinkle eggplant slices with salt and drain in colander 20 minutes. Pat dry with paper towels.

Heat oil in a skillet and add eggplant slices, a few at a time. Cook on both sides until golden. Place on paper towels to drain.

Combine remaining ingredients except lettuce and mix well. Add eggplant slices and marinate at least 30 minutes.

Line serving dish with lettuce leaves. Use slotted spoon to remove eggplant slices from dressing. Arrange over lettuce and top with walnuts.

Makes 6 servings.

Each serving contains:

Cal	Prot	Carb	Fib	Tot. Fat	Sat. Fat	Chol	Sodium
300	8g	11g	3g	27g	2g	0mg	51mg

Eggplant-Onion Salad

This is especially good with mild-flavored Vidalia onions.

1 lb. (450g) eggplant
1/4 cup (60ml) olive oil
Salt and pepper
2 onions, sliced
1 cucumber, chopped
1 red bell pepper, chopped
Chopped chives to taste
Balsamic vinegar or lemon juice (optional)

Cook whole eggplant in salted boiling water 8 minutes. Drain and cut crosswise into thin round slices.

Heat a little oil in skillet and cook eggplant a few slices at a time, adding oil as necessary. Sprinkle with salt while slices are still warm and set aside to cool and drain on paper towels.

Heat remaining oil in a separate pan and sauté onions. Drain on paper towels.

Place eggplant slices in a layer in a bowl, sprinkle with pepper and top with onions, cucumber, bell pepper and chives. Refrigerate until cold. Sprinkle with vinegar or lemon juice, if using, before serving.

Makes 6 servings.

Each serving contains:

Cal	Prot	Carb	Fib	Tot. Fat	Sat. Fat	Chol	Sodium
124	2g	10g	3g	9g	1g	0mg	49mg

Tangy Eggplant-Ham Salad

Here is an unusual warm salad, which is a good way to use leftover ham.

1 lb. (450g) eggplant, peeled
2 tomatoes, seeded and chopped
1/2 cup (125ml) cubed cooked ham
3 tablespoons (45ml) olive oil
1 teaspoon (5ml) lemon juice
Salt and pepper
1 tablespoon (15ml) chopped mint leaves
1 tablespoon (15ml) chopped parsley

Cut eggplant into 3/4-inch (2cm) cubes and cook about 15 minutes in a saucepan of boiling salted water. Drain and pat dry.

Combine remaining ingredients, pour over warm eggplant and serve.

Makes 6 servings.

Each serving contains:

Cal	Prot	Carb	Fib	Tot. Fat	Sat. Fat	Chol	Sodium
119	4g	9g	4g	8g	1g	5mg	234mg

Eggplant Terrine

("Pied-Noir" Cuisine)

The adjective *pied-noir* was applied to people of French origin living in Algeria during the 1960s. Its literal translation is "black foot."

> *1 lb. (450g) eggplant, peeled*
> *Salt*
> *3 tablespoons (45ml) olive oil*
> *4 tomatoes, peeled and chopped*
> *2 onions, chopped*
> *5 garlic cloves, chopped*
> *1/2 teaspoon (2ml) sugar*
> *Pepper to taste*

Cut eggplant into large chunks, sprinkle with salt and drain in colander 20 minutes. Pat dry with a paper towel.

Heat 1 tablespoon (15ml) oil in a heavy skillet and add eggplant, tomatoes, onions and garlic. Season with sugar, salt and pepper. Stir, cover and simmer 2 hours over very low heat.

Push mixture through a fine colander or food mill, adding remaining olive oil. Pour into a mold or terrine dish and refrigerate at least 3 hours.

Makes 6 servings.

Iranian version
Add 1 teaspoon (5ml) powdered cinnamon and 1 teaspoon (5ml) dried mint with the other seasonings.

Each serving contains:

Cal	Prot	Carb	Fib	Tot. Fat	Sat. Fat	Chol	Sodium
116	2g	13g	3g	7g	1g	0mg	55mg

Side Dishes

*I*f you're looking for something unusual to enliven an otherwise plain meal, there is a world of recipes in this chapter—Baked Eggplant with Anchovies from Italy, Ginger-Pine Nut Bake from France, Russia's Eggplant with Mint and Eggplant Masala from India.

Or, to accompany a barbecued steak or hamburgers and hot dogs, look closer to home. Mixed Grilled Vegetables can be made first and kept warm in the oven, or they can be served at room temperature.

In this chapter you will find crispy Eggplant Sticks and two kinds of fritters. For a heartier side dish, try Brown Rice Loaf or Eggplants with Brown Rice and Walnuts.

To combine all your vegetables in one dish, consider Eggplant in Vegetables Sauce, Gingered Eggplant and Green Beans, Vegetable Medley or Baked Mixed Vegetables. They're all different, and they're all good!

Spicy Indian Eggplant
(India)

The cool, creamy cucumber sauce is a perfect complement for the hot and spicy eggplant. Make it 2 to 3 hours ahead, and let the flavor develop.

> *1 lb. (450g) eggplant, cut into 1-inch (2.5cm) cubes*
> *Salt*
> *Oil for frying*
> *1-1/2 cups (375ml) all-purpose flour*
> *1/2 teaspoon (2ml) curry powder*
> *1/4 teaspoon (1ml) chili powder*
> *1 teaspoon (5ml) ground cumin*
> *1/2 cup (125ml) cold water*
> *Cucumber Sauce, below*

Sprinkle eggplant cubes with salt and drain in colander 20 minutes. Pat dry with paper towels. Heat oil in skillet.

Combine flour and spices in a bowl. Gradually pour in water, stirring constantly until smooth. Dip eggplant into batter and fry in hot oil until golden. Remove with slotted spoon and drain on paper towels.

Serve hot with cucumber sauce.

Makes 6 servings.

Each serving contains:

Cal	Prot	Carb	Fib	Tot. Fat	Sat. Fat	Chol	Sodium
234	5g	31g	3g	10g	2g	3mg	60mg

Cucumber Sauce

1 cucumber, shredded
1/2 cup (125ml) yogurt
1 teaspoon (5ml) lemon juice
2 tablespoons (30ml) chopped fresh mint

Combine all ingredients. Cover and refrigerate until needed.

Makes 1 cup (250ml).

One serving contains:

Cal	Prot	Carb	Fib	Tot. Fat	Sat. Fat	Chol	Sodium
19	1g	2g	0g	1g	1g	3mg	10mg

Eggplant Sticks

(Italy)

These deep-fried eggplant pieces may replace French fries as your favorite side dish.

1-1/2 lb. (700g) long eggplants, peeled
Salt
Oil for frying
3/4 cup (185ml) flour
1/2 teaspoon (2ml) paprika
1-1/2 cups (375ml) water
1 tablespoon (15ml) peanut oil or sunflower oil
1 tablespoon (15ml) brandy (optional)
Pepper
1 egg white, stiffly beaten
Fresh tomato salsa

Cut eggplants into sticks, 1/2 x 2 inches (1.25x5cm). Sprinkle with salt and drain in colander 20 minutes. Pat dry with paper towels. Heat oil in deep fryer.

Mix flour and paprika in a bowl, make a well and pour in water, oil and brandy, if using. Mix together, add salt and pepper to taste, and fold in beaten egg white.

Dip eggplant slices in batter. Cook in hot deep-frying oil until golden brown. Drain on paper towels. Serve very hot, with salsa.

Makes 6 servings.

Each serving contains:

Cal	Prot	Carb	Fib	Tot. Fat	Sat. Fat	Chol	Sodium
193	3g	20g	3g	12g	2g	0mg	98mg

Baked Eggplant with Anchovies

(Tuscany)

The anchovies melt into the sauce, adding a sumptuous flavor and texture.

1-1/2 lb. (700g) eggplant, cut crosswise into 1/2-inch (1.25cm)
   slices
Salt
10 anchovy fillets
Oil for frying
2 eggs, beaten
Flour for coating
12 pitted black olives, chopped
1 cup (250ml) chopped basil
1 tablespoon (15ml) dried oregano
5 oz. (145g) mozzarella cheese, sliced

Sprinkle eggplant slices with salt and drain in colander 20 minutes. Pat dry with paper towels. Soak anchovy fillets in cold water. Preheat oven to 425F (220C). Heat oil in large skillet.

Dip eggplant in beaten eggs and then in flour. Sauté in hot oil and place in colander to drain. Drain anchovies and place in blender. Add olives, basil and oregano, and purée into a paste.

In a baking dish, layer eggplant slices, anchovy mixture and cheese slices. Bake 6 to 8 minutes until cheese melts. Serve immediately.

Makes 6 servings.

Each serving contains:

Cal	Prot	Carb	Fib	Tot. Fat	Sat. Fat	Chol	Sodium
250	10g	14g	4g	18g	5g	95mg	481mg

Eggplant in Vegetable Sauce

(Italy)

Enhance seafood or pasta or other vegetables with this sauce.

1-1/2 lb. (700g) eggplant, cut lengthwise into thin slices
Salt
Olive oil
6 tomatoes, peeled and chopped
1 zucchini, sliced
3 garlic cloves, crushed
Pepper
1 recipe Onion Sauce, page 28
1 tablespoon (15ml) chopped basil
1/2 teaspoon (2ml) chopped sage leaves

Sprinkle eggplant slices with salt and drain in colander 20 minutes. Pat dry with paper towels.

Heat oil in saucepan. Sauté tomatoes and zucchini until softened. Add garlic, salt and pepper and simmer 30 minutes. Add onion sauce, basil and sage and cook 5 minutes over very low heat.

Heat oil in skillet. Sauté eggplant slices and drain on paper towels or in a colander. Place in serving dish, season lightly with salt and cover with sauce. Keep dish warm until ready to serve.

Makes 6 servings.

Each serving contains:

Cal	Prot	Carb	Fib	Tot. Fat	Sat. Fat	Chol	Sodium
216	5g	23g	6g	13g	3g	11mg	106mg

Eggplant with Potatoes

(Russia)

Dill is the secret ingredient to transform plain vegetables into a Russian favorite.

1-1/2 lb. (700g) eggplant, cut crosswise into thin slices
Salt
Oil for frying
Flour for coating
1 onion, sliced
1 green bell pepper, sliced
6 potatoes, peeled, cooked and sliced
1 recipe Béchamel Sauce, page 161
1 teaspoon (5ml) dill weed

Sprinkle eggplant slices with salt and drain in colander 20 minutes. Pat dry with paper towels. Preheat oven to 400F (200C). Grease baking dish. Heat oil in large skillet.

Dip eggplant slices into flour and fry in hot oil over high heat. Drain in a colander or on paper towels. Sauté onion and green pepper slices until onion is transparent.

Layer eggplant, potato, onions and peppers in prepared baking dish. Top with béchamel sauce, sprinkle with dill and bake in oven for 15 minutes. Serve hot.

Makes 6 servings.

Each serving contains:

Cal	Prot	Carb	Fib	Tot. Fat	Sat. Fat	Chol	Sodium
325	6g	45g	5g	15g	5g	16mg	115mg

Turkish Fritters

Hunkar Begendi

There is no need to travel to Turkey for this rich, cheesy side dish.
You can easily make it yourself an hour.

> *1-1/2 lb. (700g) eggplant*
> *2 tablespoons (30ml) butter or margarine*
> *3/4 cup (185ml) flour*
> *1 cup (250ml) milk*
> *2 eggs, beaten*
> *1/2 cup (125ml) grated Edam cheese (2 oz. / 60g)*
> *Salt and pepper to taste*
> *Oil for frying*
> *3/4 cup (185ml) breadcrumbs*

Prepare eggplant according to basic caviar recipe, page 6, preferably
over a gas flame or grill. Mash flesh with a fork.

In a heavy saucepan, melt butter and add flour, cooking gently until it
starts to brown. Add mashed eggplant and stir vigorously over low
heat. Pour in milk a little at a time, stirring constantly with a wooden
spoon. When purée is thick, add egg, cheese, salt and pepper.

Heat oil in large skillet. Form mixture into patties, coat with breadcrumbs and sauté in oil until cooked.

Makes 4 to 6 servings.

Each serving contains:

Cal	Prot	Carb	Fib	Tot. Fat	Sat. Fat	Chol	Sodium
283	9g	31g	4g	14g	6g	92mg	271mg

Indian Eggplant Purée

Garlic and ginger are often used together in East Indian cooking.
Cilantro, chili powder and turmeric add even more bite to this dish.

1-1/2 lb. (700g) eggplant
1/4 cup (60ml) melted butter or oil
2 onions, finely chopped
6 garlic cloves, crushed
2 oz. (60g) fresh ginger, grated
6 tomatoes, peeled and cubed
4 tablespoons (60ml) chopped cilantro
1/2 teaspoon (2ml) chili powder
1 teaspoon (5ml) turmeric
Salt to taste

Prepare eggplant according to basic caviar recipe, page 6. Chop
roughly with a fork.

Heat butter or oil in a heavy saucepan. Fry onions gently until
transparent. Add garlic and ginger and cook for 2 minutes, stirring
constantly. Add tomatoes, eggplant, cilantro, chili powder, turmeric
and salt. Cook 15 minutes, uncovered, over medium heat, stirring
occasionally.

Makes 6 servings.

Each serving contains:

Cal	Prot	Carb	Fib	Tot. Fat	Sat. Fat	Chol	Sodium
164	4g	21g	6g	9g	5g	21mg	148mg

Gingered Eggplant and Green Beans

Young fresh ginger, also called *spring ginger,* does not need to be peeled. The tougher skin of more mature ginger must be removed. Powdered ginger is not a good substitute for fresh.

> *1-1/2 lb. (700g) eggplant, peeled and cubed*
> *Salt*
> *1 onion, finely chopped*
> *Sunflower oil or peanut oil for sautéing*
> *2 tablespoons (30ml) grated fresh ginger*
> *1 lb. (450g) fresh green beans, sliced, or 1 pkg. (10-oz. / 280g)*
> *frozen green beans, thawed*
> *4 oz. (115g) fresh mushrooms, sliced*
> *2 eggs, beaten*
> *Pepper to taste*
> *Chopped parsley to taste*
> *Grated cheese to taste*

Sprinkle eggplant cubes with salt and drain in colander 20 minutes. Pat dry with paper towels. Preheat oven to 350F (180C).

Heat oil in ovenproof dish. Gently sauté onion until transparent. Add eggplant, ginger, green beans, mushrooms, eggs, salt and pepper. Bake in oven 30 minutes. Sprinkle with parsley and grated cheese. Return to oven for 10 minutes.

Makes 6 servings.

Each serving contains:

Cal	Prot	Carb	Fib	Tot. Fat	Sat. Fat	Chol	Sodium
149	6g	17g	6g	7g	2g	72mg	115mg

Eggplant with Roquefort

Aubergines au Roquefort
(France)

Eggplant comes in many shapes, sizes and colors. They are interchangeable in most recipes.

> *1-1/2 lb. (700g) eggplant, cut lengthwise into thin slices*
> *Salt*
> *10 oz. (280g) Roquefort or other strong blue cheese*
> *5 tablespoons (75ml) tomato paste*
> *3 garlic cloves, crushed*
> *3 tablespoons (45ml) chopped walnuts*
> *Pepper to taste*
> *Oil for frying*

Sprinkle eggplant slices with salt and drain in colander 20 minutes. Pat dry with paper towels. Preheat oven to 400F (200C).

Using a fork, cream Roquefort, tomato paste, garlic and walnuts. Season with salt and pepper.

Heat oil in a skillet and sauté eggplant slices on both sides, a few at a time. Drain on paper towels. Add more oil to pan as necessary.

In a 2-inch (5cm) deep pie plate, place eggplant and cheese mixture in alternate layers, ending with eggplant. Bake in oven 30 minutes.

Makes 6 servings.

Each serving contains:

Cal	Prot	Carb	Fib	Tot. Fat	Sat. Fat	Chol	Sodium
323	13g	12g	4g	26g	11g	43mg	1011mg

Eggplant Loaf

This dish can be served with Tomato Sauce, page 119, enhanced with a touch of garlic powder.

1 red bell pepper
2 green bell peppers, 1 chopped
1-1/2 lb. (700g) eggplant, peeled
1 onion, chopped
1 rib celery, chopped
1-2 tablespoons (15-30ml) chopped fresh cilantro
1 cup (250ml) fine breadcrumbs
2 eggs, beaten
1/2 cup (125ml) sour cream or yogurt
2 tablespoons (30ml) tomato paste
1/2 teaspoon (2ml) cumin
Nutmeg to taste
Salt and pepper to taste

Roast whole bell peppers in oven or over a grill until skins char and blister. Wrap them immediately in a paper towel or place in a plastic bag. When cool enough to handle, remove skin, stems and seeds. Dry flesh on paper towels. Cut into 1-inch (2.5cm) strips and use to decorate the bottom and sides of a lightly greased 2-inch (5cm) deep pie plate. Preheat oven to 375F (190C).

Cut eggplant into 1/2-inch (1.25cm) cubes. Boil in water to cover until tender, about 5 minutes. Drain and pat dry with paper towels. Finely chop eggplant and combine with onion, celery, cilantro, breadcrumbs, chopped bell pepper and eggs.

Blend together sour cream or yogurt and tomato paste. Stir into eggplant mixture. Add cumin, nutmeg, salt and pepper. Mix thoroughly. Pour into prepared pan. Bake in oven 30 minutes. Turn onto serving plate just before serving

Makes 6 servings.

Each serving contains:

Cal	Prot	Carb	Fib	Tot. Fat	Sat. Fat	Chol	Sodium
187	7g	26g	5g	7g	3g	79mg	273mg

Eggplants Provençal

Aubergines Provençales à la Tomate
(France)

Eggplants absorb oil greedily, so use just a little to start this dish, adding more as it is needed.

> *3 long eggplants, each 1/2 lb. (225g), halved lengthwise*
> *Olive oil for frying*
> *4 tomatoes, peeled and cubed*
> *1 onion, chopped*
> *1 shallot or green onion, minced*
> *2 garlic cloves, crushed*
> *2 teaspoons (10ml) capers*
> *1 tablespoon (15ml) red wine vinegar*
> *2 teaspoons (10ml) chopped fresh basil*
> *Salt and pepper to taste*
> *Chopped parsley*

Preheat oven to 425F (220C). With the tip of a knife, make a few cuts in eggplant skin. Heat oil in a skillet and sauté eggplants, first on the skin side, then on the cut side. Drain on paper towels.

Sauté tomatoes, onions and garlic in oil. Add capers, vinegar, basil, salt and pepper.

Arrange eggplant halves in a baking dish, cover with tomato mixture. Sprinkle with parsley. Bake in oven 15 minutes.

Makes 6 servings.

Each serving contains:

Cal	Prot	Carb	Fib	Tot. Fat	Sat. Fat	Chol	Sodium
139	2g	14g	4g	10g	1g	0mg	92mg

Eggplants with Brown Rice and Walnuts

(India)

Celery and walnuts add a satisfying crunch to this stuffing.

3 eggplants, each 1/2 lb. (225g), halved lengthwise
3 tablespoons (45ml) olive oil
1 onion, finely chopped
3 garlic cloves, crushed
1/2 lb. (225g) button mushrooms, chopped
4 ribs celery, chopped
3/4 cup (185ml) shelled walnuts, chopped
1 tablespoon (15ml) chopped parsley
2 tablespoons (30ml) tomato paste
1-2 teaspoons (5-10ml) curry powder (optional)
1/2 cup (125ml) cooked brown rice
Salt and pepper to taste
1 cup (250ml) grated cheese (4 oz. / 115g)

Preheat oven to 375F (190C). Grease cookie sheet. Place eggplants on cookie sheet, skin side up. Prick skins with a fork. Bake 30 minutes.

Heat oil in a saucepan and sauté onion gently. Add garlic, mushrooms, celery, walnuts, parsley, tomato paste and curry powder, if using. Add rice and mix thoroughly. Heat through. Season with salt and pepper and remove from heat.

When eggplants are soft, remove from oven and preheat broiler. Remove eggplant flesh with a spoon, leaving about 1/4 inch (6mm) next to skin. Mash flesh with a fork and add to rice mixture. Fill eggplant skins with stuffing and sprinkle with cheese. Place under broiler until golden, about 5 minutes

Makes 6 servings.

Each serving contains:

Cal	Prot	Carb	Fib	Tot. Fat	Sat. Fat	Chol	Sodium
311	14g	20g	5g	21g	5g	13mg	428mg

Eggplant with Lentils

Deurt Arman

(Armenia, Turkey)

Tahini quickly becomes rancid, so refrigerate or freeze it after opening and use it within a month or so.

1 lb. (450g) lentils
1-3/4 cups (440ml) thinly sliced onions
1-1/4 lb. (575g) eggplant, cut into large cubes
Salt and pepper to taste
1-1/4 cups (310ml) tahini
1 green bell pepper, chopped
4 garlic cloves, crushed
Juice of 1 lemon

Place lentils, onions and eggplant in a large pan. Cover with water and add salt and pepper. Cover and bring to a boil. Simmer 30 minutes.

Prepare sauce by combining tahini, bell pepper, garlic, lemon juice and salt. Serve vegetables cold, covered with sauce.

Makes 6 servings.

Each serving contains:

Cal	Prot	Carb	Fib	Tot. Fat	Sat. Fat	Chol	Sodium
610	32g	64g	18g	29g	4g	0mg	57mg

Eggplant Mousse

Serve this at room temperature or cold as an accompaniment to cold meat or fish.

1 lb. (450g) eggplant
2 garlic cloves, crushed
12 black olives, chopped
Juice of 1/2 lemon
Salt and pepper
1 cup (250ml) olive oil
A few basil leaves, roughly chopped
3 egg whites, stiffly beaten

Prepare eggplant according to basic caviar recipe, page 6. Mash eggplant pulp. Combine garlic, olives and lemon juice, stirring well. Add to eggplant and combine thoroughly. Season with salt and pepper. Add oil in a thin stream, beating constantly. Add basil and egg whites. Chill several hours in refrigerator.

Makes 6 servings.

Each serving contains:

Cal	Prot	Carb	Fib	Tot. Fat	Sat. Fat	Chol	Sodium
360	3g	6g	2g	37g	5g	0mg	153mg

Turkish Pilaf

Long-grain rice is preferred for this dish. Sticky rice is not acceptable in Turkey.

> *1-1/2 lb. (700g) eggplant, peeled and chopped*
> *Salt*
> *3 tablespoons (45ml) pine nuts*
> *1 tablespoon (15ml) butter*
> *1/4 cup (60ml) olive oil*
> *1 onion, finely chopped*
> *4 oz. (115g) rice, rinsed (3/4 cup / 185ml)*
> *1/2 cup (125ml) chopped parsley*
> *1-2 teaspoons (5-10ml) cinnamon*
> *1-1/2 cups (375ml) water*
> *1 large tomato, chopped*
> *1/2 to 1 cup (125-250ml) raisins*
> *Pepper*

Sprinkle eggplant with salt and drain in colander 30 minutes. Pat dry with paper towels. Sauté pine nuts in melted butter until lightly browned.

Heat oil in Dutch oven or large saucepan. Sauté onion, add eggplant and cook about 5 minutes, stirring constantly. Stir in rice, parsley and cinnamon. Pour in water and bring to a boil. Reduce heat, cover and cook about 15 minutes. Add tomato, pine nuts and raisins and cook another 5 minutes, until rice is tender. Season with salt and pepper.

Makes 6 servings.

Variation
Replace cinnamon with mint (either fresh chopped or dried and ground).

Each serving contains:

Cal	Prot	Carb	Fib	Tot. Fat	Sat. Fat	Chol	Sodium
299	5g	39g	5g	16g	3g	5mg	79mg

Ginger-Pine Nut Bake

(Nice, France)

Roast nuts by cooking quickly over high heat in a dry skillet.

1-1/2 lb. (700g) eggplant, cut into 1/2-inch (1.25cm) cubes
Salt
3 tablespoons (45ml) olive oil
1 lb. (450g) tomatoes, peeled and chopped
2 shallots or green onions, chopped
3 garlic cloves, chopped
1/4 cup (60ml) roasted pine nuts
2 tablespoons (30ml) chopped parsley
1 cup (250ml) breadcrumbs
1 tablespoon (15ml) grated fresh ginger
Pepper to taste
Pitted black olives for garnish
Roasted pine nuts for garnish, if desired

Sprinkle eggplant cubes with salt and drain in colander 20 minutes. Pat dry with paper towels. Preheat oven to 400F (200C). Grease a 9-inch-square (22.5cm) baking dish.

Heat oil in a large pan and add eggplant, tomatoes, shallots or green onions, garlic, pine nuts, parsley and breadcrumbs. Sprinkle with ginger. Season with salt and pepper and cook 2 minutes, stirring constantly.

Place in prepared baking dish and bake in oven 40 minutes. Garnish with olives and additional pine nuts, if desired.

Makes 6 servings.

Each serving contains:

Cal	Prot	Carb	Fib	Tot. Fat	Sat. Fat	Chol	Sodium
236	6g	26g	5g	14g	2g	0mg	266mg

Aromatic Italian Eggplants

(Sicily)

This dish can also be served cold as a starter.

> *3 Asian or Oriental eggplants, each 1/2 lb. (225g), halved*
>   *lengthwise*
> *Salt*
> *Olive oil*
> *2 tablespoons (30ml) chopped parsley*
> *1 cup (250ml) chopped fresh basil leaves*
> *2 tablespoons (30ml) chopped fresh rosemary*
> *6 garlic cloves, chopped*
> *Pepper to taste*
> *1 cup (250ml) tomato sauce*

Sprinkle eggplant with salt and drain in colander 20 minutes. Pat dry with paper towels. Preheat broiler.

Place eggplant halves in baking dish, cut side up. Brush with oil. Broil until golden. Lower oven temperature to 375F (190C).

Combine parsley, basil, rosemary and garlic.

With a sharp knife, make several cuts in eggplant flesh. Insert a little herb mixture into each cut. Season with salt and pepper. Spoon tomato sauce over eggplants. Return to oven and bake about 30 minutes.

Makes 6 servings.

Each serving contains:

Cal	Prot	Carb	Fib	Tot. Fat	Sat. Fat	Chol	Sodium
131	2g	12g	4g	9g	1g	0mg	296mg

Tomato Eggplant Curry

Baigan Tamatar
(India)

In Indian cooking, it is the variety of spices that makes the dish. This one is no exception.

> *1-3/4 lb. (800g) eggplant, cut into 1-inch (2.5cm) cubes*
> *Salt*
> *1/2 cup (125ml) melted butter or oil*
> *2 medium onions, finely chopped*
> *1 garlic clove, chopped*
> *1 teaspoon (5ml) chili powder*
> *1-2 teaspoons (5-10ml) curry powder*
> *1 bay leaf*
> *2-inch (5cm) cinnamon stick*
> *2 teaspoons (10ml) ground coriander*
> *1 teaspoon (5ml) pepper*
> *1-3/4 lb. (800g) tomatoes*
> *4 teaspoons (20ml) tomato paste*
> *1/2 cup (125ml) water*

Sprinkle eggplant with salt and drain in colander 20 minutes. Pat dry with paper towels.

Heat butter or oil in a heavy saucepan over low heat. Gently sauté onions 2 to 3 minutes. Add garlic, chili powder, curry powder, bay leaf, cinnamon, coriander, 1 teaspoon (5ml) salt and pepper. Cook 2 to 3 minutes, stirring occasionally.

Add tomatoes, stir and bring to a boil, adding a little extra water, if necessary.

Add eggplant cubes, turning to coat with mixture. Add tomato paste and water. Cover and simmer 30 minutes or until eggplant is soft. Eggplant should retain its shape, while tomatoes should be reduced to a pulp. Sauce should be quite thick. If there is still a little water left at the end of the cooking time, raise the heat and cook uncovered until it has evaporated. Remove and discard bay leaf and cinnamon stick.

Makes 6 servings.

Each serving contains:

Cal	Prot	Carb	Fib	Tot. Fat	Sat. Fat	Chol	Sodium
222	4g	20g	6g	16g	10g	41mg	252mg

Eggplant with Tamarind

Baigan Bhagar

(India)

Here is a dish with a very particular and interesting flavor, the tamarind serves to soften the naturally spicy taste of the eggplant. Look for tamarind near the dried chile peppers and spices in your supermarket.

1/2 cup (125ml) boiling water
2 oz. (60g) tamarind
1-3/4 lb. (800g) eggplant, cut into 1-inch (2.5cm) cubes
Salt
1/2 cup (125ml) melted butter or oil
1 onion, finely chopped
2 garlic cloves, finely chopped
1-1/2 teaspoons (7ml) chili powder
2 teaspoons (10ml) ground coriander
2 teaspoons (10ml) turmeric
Pinch of saffron powder
2 teaspoons (10ml) mustard seeds
2 bay leaves
1 cup (250ml) shredded coconut
2 teaspoons (10ml) honey
2 teaspoons (10ml) garam masala
2 green chile peppers, chopped

Pour boiling water over tamarind and soak 2 hours. Sprinkle eggplant with salt and drain in colander 20 minutes. Pat dry with paper towels.

Heat butter or oil in large, heavy-based saucepan and sauté eggplant cubes gently 1 to 2 minutes. Remove from pan with a slotted spoon and set aside.

Adding more butter or oil, if necessary, sauté onion until transparent. Add garlic, chili powder, coriander, turmeric, saffron, mustard seeds, bay leaves and coconut. Add tamarind soaking water. Press tamarind pulp against side of pan to extract all its juice. Discard tamarind pulp.

Add honey, mix well and stir in eggplant. Sprinkle with salt. Cover tightly and simmer 5 minutes. Add garam masala and chile peppers and mix well. Simmer, covered, 15 minutes. Check occasionally that eggplants are not sticking, turning them carefully so as not to break them. Remove and discard bay leaves before serving.

Makes 6 servings.

Each serving contains:

Cal	Prot	Carb	Fib	Tot. Fat	Sat. Fat	Chol	Sodium
284	3g	25g	7g	21g	14g	41mg	221mg

Vegetable Medley

Ragout d'Aubergines
(Provence)

Herbes de Provence is an assortment of herbs, including thyme, summer savory, rosemary, bay leaves. It is usually sold in bunches, but can also be found dried and bottled.

> *1-1/2 lb. (700g) eggplant, cut into large cubes*
> *Salt*
> *5 oz. (145g) bacon, diced*
> *1/4 cup (60ml) olive oil*
> *2 onions, finely chopped*
> *1 green bell pepper, sliced*
> *1/2 lb. (225g) fresh green beans, sliced*
> *2 carrots, thinly sliced*
> *6 large ripe tomatoes, peeled and cubed*
> *4 large garlic cloves, crushed*
> *Bunch of herbes de Provence, or 2 teaspoons (10ml) dried*
> *1-1/2 cups (375ml) dry white wine*
> *Pepper to taste*
> *1/2 cup chopped parsley*

Sprinkle eggplant with salt and drain in colander 20 minutes. Pat dry with paper towels.

In a large pan, fry bacon in olive oil. Add eggplant cubes and cook gently, stirring constantly. Add a little more oil if necessary. Add onions, bell pepper, green beans and carrots. Mix together. When vegetables begin to soften, add tomatoes, garlic, herbs, wine, salt and pepper. Cover and simmer over low heat 30 to 40 minutes.

Sprinkle with parsley just before serving.

Makes 6 servings.

Variation
Omit bell pepper, beans and carrots. Add 1 package (16-oz. / 450g) frozen mixed vegetables.

Each serving contains:

Cal	Prot	Carb	Fib	Tot. Fat	Sat. Fat	Chol	Sodium
227	7g	26g	8g	14g	3g	7mg	249mg

Layered Tomato, Cheese and Eggplant

(Armenia)

This hearty side dish is a good accompaniment for broiled or roast meat. Omit potatoes and serve a fruit salad for contrast.

4 eggs, beaten
4 cups (1 liter) grated Gruyère or Parmesan cheese (1 lb. / 450g)
Salt and pepper to taste
1-1/2 lb. (700g) eggplant, cut crosswise into 1/2-inch (1.25cm)
   slices
Butter to taste
4 tomatoes, sliced and seeded
Chopped oregano to taste
Chopped walnuts for garnish

Preheat oven to 375F (190C). Grease a baking dish. Combine eggs, cheese, salt and pepper.

In prepared dish, spread a layer of eggplant slices. Pour over a little egg-cheese mixture and dot with butter. Cover with a layer of tomatoes. Repeat layers, finishing with tomatoes. Sprinkle with oregano.

Bake 1 hour. Garnish with walnuts and serve.

Makes 6 servings.

Each serving contains:

Cal	Prot	Carb	Fib	Tot. Fat	Sat. Fat	Chol	Sodium
513	30g	13g	4g	39g	20g	246mg	430mg

Mixed Grilled Vegetables

(United States)

With the popularity of both indoor and outdoor grilling, here is the ideal dish to accompany beef or chicken.

2 Japanese eggplants, each 3/4 lb. (340g), cut lengthwise into
1/4-inch (6mm) slices
1 red bell pepper, quartered and seeded
1 green bell pepper, quartered and seeded
2 zucchini, cut diagonally into 1/4-inch (6mm) slices
1/4 lb. (115g) whole fresh mushrooms
Pine nuts for garnish

Marinade:
3/4 cup (185ml) olive oil or vegetable oil
6 tablespoons (90ml) red-wine vinegar
1 garlic clove, minced
1 tablespoon (15ml) chopped fresh oregano, or 1 teaspoon (5ml)
dried
Salt and pepper to taste

Place all vegetables in large bowl. Combine marinade ingredients and pour over vegetables. Toss to coat. Let stand 10 to 15 minutes.

Preheat grill or broiler. Thread peppers, zucchini and mushrooms onto skewers and place with eggplant slices on grill or oiled broiler rack. You can also use a vegetable basket for the grill instead of skewers. Cook about 5 minutes and turn. Continue cooking and turning until tender and lightly charred. Eggplant will be done first. Bell pepper skins should be blistered and charred. Remove peppers and scrape off charred skin.

Place all vegetables on platter. Drizzle with remaining marinade. Sprinkle with pine nuts. Serve hot or at room temperature.

Makes 6 to 8 servings.

Each serving contains:

Cal	Prot	Carb	Fib	Tot. Fat	Sat. Fat	Chol	Sodium
345	4g	15g	5g	32g	4g	0mg	51mg

Braised Eggplant and Chiles

Baigan Bhugia
(India)

This dish uses a very simple cooking method: the vegetables are cooked in as little liquid as possible, thus retaining the maximum flavor. Keep a close eye on the cooking, to ensure that the vegetables do not dry out or burn.

> *1/4 cup (185ml) melted butter or oil*
> *2 large onions, finely chopped*
> *1 teaspoon (5ml) salt*
> *2 teaspoons (10ml) paprika*
> *1-1/2 lb. (700g) eggplant, cut into 1/2-inch (1.25cm) cubes*
> *1/4 cup (60ml) tomato sauce*
> *1-3 green chile peppers, finely chopped*
> *2 teaspoons (10ml) garam masala*

Heat butter or oil in a thick-based saucepan. Add onions and sauté gently. Add salt and paprika to the pan and mix well. Add eggplant cubes and tomato sauce, turning eggplant to coat with sauce. Heat should be quite high, but watch that eggplant does not stick. If necessary, add water.

Add chile peppers. Cover, reduce heat and simmer gently about 5 minutes. Stir in garam masala and cook about 15 minutes or until eggplant is soft.

Makes 6 servings.

Each serving contains:

Cal	Prot	Carb	Fib	Tot. Fat	Sat. Fat	Chol	Sodium
138	2g	16g	5g	8g	5g	21mg	504mg

Pakistani-Style Eggplant
Bengan Curry

A delightful blend of aromatic spices enlivens this dish.

Sunflower oil
1 onion, finely chopped
2 large tomatoes, peeled and chopped
2 garlic cloves, crushed
1/2 teaspoon (2ml) ground ginger
1/2 teaspoon (2ml) ground cumin
2 teaspoons (10ml) curry powder
1 teaspoon (5ml) turmeric
1 teaspoon (5ml) coriander seeds
Salt and pepper to taste
1-1/2 lb. (700g) eggplant, cut crosswise into thin slices
2 green bell peppers, cut into thin slices.

Heat oil and sauté onion. Add tomatoes, garlic and spices and mix well. Add eggplant and peppers. Cook over very low heat, stirring occasionally, about 20 minutes

Makes 6 servings.

Each serving contains:

Cal	Prot	Carb	Fib	Tot. Fat	Sat. Fat	Chol	Sodium
145	2g	14g	5g	10g	1g	0mg	55mg

Spicy West Indian Eggplant

Aubergines Sauce au Chile

Steaming the eggplant ahead of time will reduce the amount of oil needed.

1-1/2 lb. (700g) eggplant, peeled
Salt
1 onion, finely chopped
3 tablespoons (45ml) oil
3 garlic cloves, minced
1/2 teaspoon (2ml) dried thyme leaves
1/2 teaspoon (2ml) dried oregano leaves
Chile pepper flakes (optional)
2-3 fresh green chile peppers, seeded and chopped
Pepper
1 avocado
1-2 tablespoons (15-30ml) lemon juice

Cut eggplant crosswise into 1/2-inch (1.25cm) slices. Sprinkle with salt and drain in colander 20 minutes. Pat dry with paper towels.

Sauté onion in oil until transparent. Add garlic, herbs, chile peppers, salt and pepper and stir over low heat. Add eggplant slices, with a little more oil, if necessary. Simmer 25 minutes over low heat, stirring regularly.

Peel and chop avocado. Mix with lemon juice. Garnish eggplant dish with avocado and serve hot.

Makes 6 servings.

Each serving contains:

Cal	Prot	Carb	Fib	Tot. Fat	Sat. Fat	Chol	Sodium
166	2g	15g	5g	12g	2g	0mg	54mg

Eggplant with Mint

I Mizizani Incu a Menta

(Russia)

If you're short of time, you could use slices of eggplant instead of sticks. Be sure they are well cooked before serving.

> *1-1/2 lb. (700g) eggplant, cut into sticks, 1/2 x 2 inches*
> *(1.25x5cm)*
> *Salt*
> *Oil for frying*
> *2 eggs, beaten*
> *1-1/2 cups (375ml) seasoned breadcrumbs*
> *1 cup Tomato Sauce, page 119*
> *2 tablespoons (30ml) chopped fresh mint*

Sprinkle eggplant sticks with salt and drain in colander 20 minutes. Pat dry with paper towels.

Heat oil to 350F (175C) in deep-fryer or large saucepan. Dip eggplant sticks in beaten eggs and roll in crumbs. Fry until golden, turning to cook all sides. Heat sauce and pour over. Sprinkle with mint.

Makes 6 servings.

Each serving contains:

Cal	Prot	Carb	Fib	Tot. Fat	Sat. Fat	Chol	Sodium
277	8g	34g	4g	13g	2g	71mg	979mg

Eggplant with Sugar Peas and Ginger
(China)

Salting eggplant shortens the cooking time, making it a good candidate for a stir-fry.

> *1-1/2 lb. (700g) eggplant, cut into 1-inch (2.5cm) cubes*
> *Salt*
> *3 tablespoons (45ml) vegetable oil*
> *2 tablespoons (30ml) grated fresh ginger*
> *3 green onions, chopped*
> *1 fresh chile pepper, chopped, or 1/2 teaspoon (2ml) chili sauce*
> *1 cup (250ml) sugar peas*
> *1 teaspoon (5ml) sugar*
> *4 tablespoons (60ml) soy sauce*
> *3/4 cup (185ml) vegetable or chicken stock*
> *2 tablespoons (30ml) sherry or white wine*
> *Pepper to taste*

Sprinkle eggplant cubes with salt and drain in colander 20 minutes.

Heat oil in wok or large skillet. Sauté ginger and onions. Add eggplant and chile pepper or chili sauce and stir-fry until lightly browned. Stir in peas.

Stir sugar and soy sauce into stock and pour over eggplant mixture. Continue to cook and stir until liquid is absorbed. Drizzle sherry or wine over all and toss. Season with salt and pepper. Serve at once.

Makes 6 servings.

Each serving contains:

Cal	Prot	Carb	Fib	Tot. Fat	Sat. Fat	Chol	Sodium
128	4g	14g	5g	7g	1g	0mg	930mg

Eggplant Masala

Baigan Masala
(India)

For this dish, which combines frying and steaming techniques, be sure to watch carefully and to use as little liquid as possible.

Juice of 1 lemon
2 tablespoons (30ml) vinegar
2 teaspoons (10ml) chili powder
2 teaspoons (10ml) ground ginger
2 teaspoons (10ml) garam masala
2 teaspoons (10ml) pepper
1 teaspoon (5ml) turmeric
2/3 cup (160ml) grated coconut
2 lb. (900g) long eggplants, cut crosswise into 1/2-inch
   (1.25cm) slices
1/2 cup (125ml) melted butter or oil
1 medium onion, finely chopped
2 garlic cloves, finely chopped
Salt

Combine lemon juice, vinegar, chili powder, ginger, garam masala, pepper, turmeric and coconut. Stir for a few minutes to make a thick spicy sauce—the masala.

Place eggplant slices on a dish and cover them with sauce. Set aside for 30 minutes until well marinated.

Heat butter or oil in a heavy saucepan. Cook onion and garlic gently until transparent. Add eggplant and masala. Season with salt. Cover pan with a close-fitting lid and cook over low heat 20 minutes, checking occasionally to see that the eggplant does not dry out. If necessary, turn slices over, but be careful not to break them. Serve as soon as eggplant is tender.

Makes 6 servings.

Each serving contains:

Cal	Prot	Carb	Fib	Tot. Fat	Sat. Fat	Chol	Sodium
234	2g	17g	6g	19g	12g	41mg	218mg

Chickpeas and Eggplant

(Arab Cuisine)

Use any proportion of eggplant to chickpeas that appeals to you.

1-1/2 lb. (700g) eggplant, cut into 1-inch (2.5cm) cubes
Salt
3 tablespoons (45ml) olive oil
8 garlic cloves, crushed
2 green onions, chopped
1 can (15-oz. / 425g) chickpeas or garbanzo beans, drained
1-2 teaspoons (5-10ml) chili powder
1 tablespoon (15ml) chopped parsley
Pepper

Sprinkle eggplant cubes with salt and drain in colander 20 minutes. Pat dry with paper towels.

Heat oil in a large saucepan or skillet and sauté eggplant, garlic and onions. Add chickpeas or garbanzos and chili powder. Cover and simmer until eggplant is tender. Sprinkle with parsley. Season with salt and pepper to taste.

Makes 6 servings.

Each serving contains:

Cal	Prot	Carb	Fib	Tot. Fat	Sat. Fat	Chol	Sodium
186	5g	26g	6g	8g	1g	0mg	270mg

Baked Mixed Vegetables

Almonds add a nice crunch to this tasty vegetable combination.

3/4 lb. (340g) long eggplants
10 oz. (280g) medium-sized zucchini
1 lb. 2 oz. (500g) firm ripe tomatoes, sliced, drained and seeded
1/4 lb. (115g) button mushrooms, very thinly sliced
1/4 cup (60ml) slivered blanched almonds
Salt and pepper
Thyme
2 garlic cloves, crushed
2 tablespoons (30ml) olive oil

Preheat oven to 400F (200C). Grease a baking dish.

Remove stems from eggplants and peel, leaving strips of black and white. Cut off ends of zucchini. Peel in strips like eggplants and cut both into very thin slices.

In prepared baking dish, alternate vegetables in overlapping rows, sprinkling each layer with almonds. Season with salt and pepper, sprinkle with thyme and garlic and top with olive oil. Cover, place in oven and bake 30 to 45 minutes.

Makes 6 servings.

Each serving contains:

Cal	Prot	Carb	Fib	Tot. Fat	Sat. Fat	Chol	Sodium
112	3g	11g	4g	7g	1g	0mg	57mg

Herbed Eggplant and Tomatoes

Banjan Boroni

(Afghanistan)

Serve this dish of eggplant with tomatoes and yogurt the next time you have guests.

> *1-1/2 lb. (700g) eggplant, cut lengthwise into slices*
> *Oil for sautéing*
> *3 tomatoes, chopped*
> *20 oz. (575g) yogurt*
> *3 garlic cloves, crushed*
> *Salt and pepper to taste*
> *1 tablespoon (15ml) chopped mint*
> *1 tablespoon (15ml) chopped marjoram*

Sauté eggplant slices in hot oil until tender. Set aside. Sauté tomatoes separately in same oil.

Combine yogurt and garlic. Season with salt and pepper.

Alternate layers of tomatoes and eggplant in a serving dish. Season each layer with mint, marjoram, salt and pepper and keep warm.

Pour a few spoonfuls of yogurt onto the vegetables; serve the rest in a separate bowl.

Makes 6 servings.

Each serving contains:

Cal	Prot	Carb	Fib	Tot. Fat	Sat. Fat	Chol	Sodium
187	5g	16g	4g	13g	3g	12mg	100mg

Brown Rice Loaf

A hearty loaf packed with nutrition and a variety of textures.

1-1/2 lb. (700g) eggplant, peeled and cut crosswise into thin slices
Salt
Sunflower oil for frying
3 tomatoes, peeled, seeded and chopped
1 onion, finely chopped
Pepper to taste
1 tablespoon (15ml) chopped parsley
3 eggs, beaten
1/2 cup (125ml) sour cream
Grated nutmeg
1/2 cup (125ml) shredded Cheddar cheese (2 oz. / 60g)
9 oz. (250g) brown rice, cooked and cooled
1/4 cup (60ml) pine nuts
1/4 cup (60ml) raisins

Sprinkle eggplant slices with salt and drain in colander 20 minutes. Pat dry with paper towels. Preheat oven to 400F (200C). Grease a loaf pan.

Heat 1 tablespoon (15ml) oil in saucepan or skillet. Add tomatoes and onion and cook 3 minutes, stirring constantly. Then add parsley, season with salt and pepper and remove from heat

Heat more oil in another pan and cook eggplant slices gently, a few at a time. Remove to paper towels to drain.

Combine eggs, sour cream, salt, pepper and nutmeg. Add cheese, rice, pine nuts and raisins.

In prepared pan, alternate layers of eggplant slices and rice mixture, finishing with eggplant. Cover with tomato mixture. Bake 30 to 40 minutes.

Makes 6 servings.

Each serving contains:

Cal	Prot	Carb	Fib	Tot. Fat	Sat. Fat	Chol	Sodium
372	12g	31g	6g	25g	7g	125mg	161mg

Eggplant Fritters

These delicacies cook quickly—and disappear quickly, too.

> *1-1/2 lb. (700g) eggplant, cubed*
> *3 bacon slices, cooked and crumbled*
> *2 green onions, chopped*
> *5 tablespoons (75ml) chopped, drained sun-dried tomatoes*
> *2 tablespoons (30ml) chopped parsley*
> *2 eggs, beaten*
> *3/4 cup (185ml) fresh breadcrumbs*
> *1/2 teaspoon (2ml) baking powder*
> *3/4 cup (185ml) flour*
> *1/2 teaspoon (2ml) basil*
> *1 teaspoon (5ml) dried mint*
> *Oil*
> *1/2 teaspoon (2ml) basil*
> *3/4 cup (185ml) sour cream*

Cook eggplant in boiling water 5 to 8 minutes until tender. Drain well and press out excess liquid. Finely chop by hand or pulse briefly in food processor. In a bowl, combine eggplant with remaining ingredients except oil, basil and sour cream. Stir basil into sour cream.

Heat about 1 inch (2.5cm) oil in a large skillet. Spoon about 2 tablespoons (30ml) eggplant mixture into oil. Press lightly to form fritter. When edges begin to brown, turn and press again. Cook other side. Remove and place on paper towel to drain, covering to keep warm. Repeat with remaining batter, adding more oil if needed.

Serve fritters topped with basil-flavored sour cream.

Makes 8 servings.

Each serving contains:

Cal	Prot	Carb	Fib	Tot. Fat	Sat. Fat	Chol	Sodium
226	6g	20g	3g	15g	5g	65mg	168mg

Vegetarian Main Dishes

*E*ggplant is a natural for vegetarians and for any-one else who wants to cook nutritious main dishes with a difference. In this chapter you will find several old favorites—Ratatouille Niçoise, Vegetarian Lasagna, Eggplant Parmigiana and Vegetarian Moussaka.

As you might expect, most of the recipes combine eggplant with other vegetables. Some have costar-ring roles, as in Eggplant with Tomatoes, Eggplant and Zucchini Loaf and Eggplant-Mushroom Stir-Fry. Others appear without fanfare—artichokes in Pizza and Eggplant Bohemian, fresh green beans and peas in New Delhi Stuffed Eggplants, and sweet potato in Eggplant Tempura.

Double-Curry Eggplant is an exotic delight. Eggplant Gratin will be appreciated by the not-so-adventurous. Eggplant and Pasta is not as highly seasoned as many dishes, but its subtle flavors blend into a mouth-watering entrée.

Just look them over. You'll want to try them all!

Eggplant Gratin
Gratin d'Aubergines
(Provence)

For a nice finishing touch, sprinkle with toasted sesame seeds just before serving.

2 lb. (900g) eggplant, peeled, if desired
Salt
Oil for frying
2 lb. (900g) tomatoes, peeled, seeded and chopped
1 tablespoon (15ml) olive oil
2 tablespoons (30ml) chopped basil
1 tablespoon (15ml) chopped parsley
1 teaspoon (5ml) thyme
4 garlic cloves, crushed
Pepper to taste
1-3/4 cups (440ml) grated Gruyère cheese (7 oz. / 200g)

Cut eggplant lengthwise into very thin slices. Sprinkle with salt and drain in colander 20 minutes. Pat dry with paper towels. Heat oil in deep fryer or skillet.

Fry eggplant slices a few at a time in hot oil. Cook until just golden and drain on paper towels.

Place tomatoes in a saucepan with olive oil, basil, parsley, thyme, garlic, salt and pepper. Cook over high heat to evaporate liquid, lower heat and simmer about 10 minutes. Mash with a fork or in blender or food processor.

Preheat broiler. In a baking dish, alternate layers of eggplant, grated cheese and tomato mixture, ending with a layer of cheese. Place under broiler until cheese melts.

Makes 6 servings.

Variations

1. Omit cheese and top with a mixture of breadcrumbs, chopped garlic and parsley. Place in 375F (190C) oven so breadcrumbs do not burn.

2. Replace grated cheese with thin slices of mozzarella.

3. Pour in 4 beaten eggs just before placing in oven.

4. Alternate eggplant with layers of sliced zucchini and thin strips of red or green pepper.

Each serving contains:

Cal	Prot	Carb	Fib	Tot. Fat	Sat. Fat	Chol	Sodium
305	12g	17g	5g	22g	8g	35mg	214mg

Eggplant with Tomatoes

Lou Tchacho

(Haute Provence)

Green olives and lots of garlic add a special touch to this dish.

2 lb. (900g) tomatoes, quartered and seeded
1/2 cup (125ml) green olives, sliced
6 garlic cloves, crushed
1 tablespoon (15ml) chopped parsley
A few sage leaves
1 bay leaf
Salt and pepper to taste
Olive oil for sautéing
1-1/2 lb. (700g) eggplant, peeled and cut crosswise into thick
  slices
4 teaspoons (20ml) sugar

Place tomatoes in a heavy saucepan. Add olives, garlic, parsley, sage, bay leaf, salt and pepper. Cook uncovered over low heat, stirring occasionally, until purée is quite thick.

Heat oil in skillet. Gently sauté eggplant slices. Drain on paper towels.

Stir sugar into tomato purée. Add eggplant and cook, uncovered, over very low heat 45 to 60 minutes. Mixture should become slightly caramelized, but should not stick to pan. Remove and discard bay leaf before serving. Serve hot.

Makes 6 servings.

Each serving contains:

Cal	Prot	Carb	Fib	Tot. Fat	Sat. Fat	Chol	Sodium
163	3g	18g	4g	10g	1g	0mg	187mg

Eggplant Bohemian

Bohemienne

(Provence)

It is perfectly acceptable to use canned tomatoes if you are feeling pressed for time.

1-1/2 lb. (700g) eggplant, peeled
Salt
5 tablespoons (75ml) olive oil
1 onion, finely chopped
1-1/2 lb. (700g) tomatoes, peeled and cubed
1 pkg. (10-oz. / 280g) frozen artichokes, thawed
3 garlic cloves, crushed
2 tablespoons (30ml) chopped parsley
Pepper to taste
Herbes de Provence to taste
1-1/4 cups (310ml) grated Parmesan cheese (5 oz. / 145g)

Cut eggplant crosswise into 1/2-inch (1.25cm) slices Sprinkle with salt and drain in colander 20 minutes. Pat dry with paper towels.

Heat oil in heavy skillet and sauté onion slowly until transparent. Add eggplant and cook gently. Add tomatoes, artichokes, garlic and parsley. Season with salt, pepper and herbes de Provence. Cover and simmer 15 to 20 minutes. Remove cover and cook until excess liquid has evaporated. Sprinkle with grated cheese. Serve hot.

Makes 6 servings.

Each serving contains:

Cal	Prot	Carb	Fib	Tot. Fat	Sat. Fat	Chol	Sodium
283	12g	21g	7g	18g	6g	16mg	518mg

Ratatouille Niçoise

(France)

This popular main dish from Provence has as many variations as there are cooks, and it can be used in many ways. It makes a delicious starter, served cold and garnished with anchovies or surrounded by thin slices of ham. It is good as a stuffing for other vegetables, such as tomatoes, or as a filling for an omelet.

1-1/2 lb. (700g) eggplant, cut into large cubes
1/2 cup (125ml) olive oil
2-1/4 lb. (1 kg) tomatoes, peeled and cubed
3 green bell peppers, cut into thin strips
1 onion, finely chopped
4 large garlic cloves, crushed
2 bay leaves
3 zucchini, sliced
Fresh thyme to taste
Salt and pepper to taste

Sprinkle eggplant cubes with salt and drain in colander 20 minutes. Pat dry with paper towels. Heat 3 tablespoons oil in heavy pan and sauté tomatoes, peppers, onion and garlic, stirring occasionally. Add bay leaves and simmer until water evaporates. Remove from heat.

Heat remaining oil in a second pan and cook eggplant and zucchini over high heat. Stir occasionally. When vegetables soften, reduce heat, add sprigs of thyme and simmer uncovered for 20 minutes, stirring occasionally.

Add tomato mixture, season with salt and pepper and simmer, partly covered, 30 minutes. Stir occasionally. Remove and discard bay leaves.

Makes 6 servings.

Cooking Variations

1. No-Fuss Method—Prepare vegetables. Heat oil in a large saucepan. Add all ingredients and mix well. Cook over high heat about 10 minutes. Lower heat and simmer uncovered approximately 1 hour. Stir occasionally, adding tomato juice, if necessary, to prevent sticking. Remove and discard bay leaves.

2. Oven Method—Preheat oven to 375F (190C). Prepare vegetables. Pour everything except olive oil into a large casserole dish. Add 2 tablespoons olive oil and cook in oven 1 to 1-1/2 hours, stirring occasionally, until vegetables are golden. If necessary, moisten with tomato juice and cover. Remove and discard bay leaves. Prepared this way, the vegetables will retain their shape.

Ingredient Variations

1. Instead of fresh tomatoes, use 1 can (28 oz. / 800g) whole tomatoes with their juice. Chop tomatoes with a fork.

2. Add chopped parsley, fresh basil or chile peppers.

3. Add mushrooms.

Each serving contains:

Cal	Prot	Carb	Fib	Tot. Fat	Sat. Fat	Chol	Sodium
295	6g	31g	9g	19g	3g	0mg	72mg

Eggplant and Zucchini Loaf

Like ratatouille, this loaf can be served cold and makes a very good first course.

1 onion, chopped
4 garlic cloves, crushed
2 tablespoons (30ml) chopped parsley
Herbes de Provence to taste
1/2 cup (125ml) olive oil
1 lb. 2 oz. (500g) eggplant, unpeeled, sliced lengthwise
14 oz. (400g) zucchini, sliced, unpeeled
1 lb. 5 oz. (600g) tomatoes, peeled and sliced
Salt and pepper to taste
Fresh basil, or 1 green or red bell pepper

Preheat oven to 375F (190C). Grease a 2-inch (5cm) deep pie plate. Combine onion, garlic, parsley and herbes de Provence.

Heat oil in a large skillet and sauté eggplant slices on both sides. Drain on paper towels. Add more oil as required.

Spread a layer of eggplant slices in prepared pie plate, overlapping a little. Top with layers of onion mixture, zucchini and tomatoes. Repeat layers, ending with eggplant. Season with salt and pepper. Cover with foil, cut a few steam holes in foil, and bake in oven 45 minutes.

To serve, turn onto a hot serving plate and garnish with basil or rings of bell pepper.

Makes 6 servings.

Each serving contains:

Cal	Prot	Carb	Fib	Tot. Fat	Sat. Fat	Chol	Sodium
222	3g	14g	4g	19g	3g	0mg	60mg

Vegetable-Stuffed Eggplants

Keema Baigan
(India)

Traditionally, *keema* is a ground-meat curry. In this recipe, the *baigani* (eggplants) are stuffed with a vegetable mixture.

> *3 eggplants, each 1/2 lb. (225g), halved lengthwise*
> *2 quarts (2 liters) water*
> *1/2 cup (125ml) melted butter or cooking oil*
> *1 onion, sliced*
> *2/3 cup (160ml) peas*
> *2/3 cup (160ml) sliced carrots*
> *7 oz. (200g) tomatoes, peeled and cubed*
> *1/2 teaspoon (2ml) turmeric*
> *1 teaspoon (5ml) ground coriander*
> *1/4 teaspoon (1ml) chili powder*
> *1 teaspoon (5ml) paprika*
> *1 teaspoon (5ml) salt*
> *1 teaspoon (5ml) black pepper*
> *1-inch (2.5cm) piece of fresh ginger, peeled*

Boil eggplants in water 10 to 15 minutes. Remove from water with a slotted spoon. Remove flesh with a spoon, leaving a 1/4-inch (6mm) layer next to skin. Mash flesh. Set aside skins and flesh. Preheat oven to 350F (180C).

Heat butter or oil in a large skillet. Sauté onion. Add peas and carrots and cook over low heat until tender. Add eggplant, tomatoes, turmeric, coriander, chili powder, paprika, salt and pepper and mix well. Cook until tomatoes are tender.

Cut ginger into very thin strips. Place eggplant skins on a baking sheet. Add ginger to cooked vegetables and fill eggplant skins with mixture. Bake until filling is just golden, about 30 minutes.

Makes 6 servings.

Each serving contains:

Cal	Prot	Carb	Fib	Tot. Fat	Sat. Fat	Chol	Sodium
211	3g	17g	5g	16g	10g	41mg	539mg

New Delhi Stuffed Eggplants

Baigan Ka Tikka
(India)

Don't be frightened off by the long list of ingredients. The final result is worth the effort.

> *3 eggplants, each 1/2 lb. (225g), halved lengthwise*
> *Salt*
> *1/4 cup (60ml) melted butter or oil*
> *2 garlic cloves, crushed*
> *1 teaspoon (5ml) grated fresh ginger*
> *1 onion, finely chopped*
> *1 teaspoon (5ml) ground coriander*
> *1 teaspoon (5ml) garam masala*
> *1/4 lb. (115g) fresh green beans, sliced*
> *1/2 lb. (250g) fresh peas*
> *1 carrot, finely chopped*
> *1 large potato, finely chopped*
> *2 tomatoes, finely chopped*
> *1 tablespoon (15ml) chopped fresh mint*
> *3 tablespoons (45ml) chopped fresh cilantro*
> *3 tablespoons (45ml) all-purpose flour*
> *5 tablespoons (75ml) water*
> *1/2 teaspoon (2ml) ground cumin*
> *1/4 teaspoon (1ml) chili powder*

Remove eggplant flesh with a spoon, leaving a 1/4-inch (6mm) layer next to skin. Sprinkle skins with salt and drain 20 minutes. Chop the flesh.

Heat 1 tablespoon butter or oil in heavy pan. Sauté garlic, ginger and onion gently, stirring constantly, 1 minute. Add coriander, garam masala and salt to taste. Add eggplant flesh and cook gently 7 minutes, stirring regularly. Add green beans, peas, carrot, potato and tomatoes. Mix well, cover and simmer 5 minutes. Add mint and cilantro.

Preheat oven to 375F (190C). Grease baking sheet. Rinse eggplant skins, dry carefully and fill with vegetable mixture, packing down firmly. Combine flour, water, cumin and chili powder to make batter. Cover eggplant halves with batter.

Heat remaining butter or oil in skillet and add eggplant boats, stuffed side down. Sauté 2 minutes. When golden, place on prepared baking sheet, stuffed side up. Bake 25 minutes and serve hot.

Makes 6 servings.

Each serving contains:

Cal	Prot	Carb	Fib	Tot. Fat	Sat. Fat	Chol	Sodium
209	5g	28g	7g	10g	1g	0mg	65mg

Eggplants Stuffed with Rice and Cheddar

The long cooking time gives the flavors time to blend.

3 eggplants, each 1/2 lb. (225g), halved lengthwise
5 tablespoons (75ml) olive oil
3 green bell peppers, cut into cubes
1 rib of celery, cut into cubes
1 onion, finely chopped
1 cup (250ml) long-grain rice
2 lb. (900g) tomatoes, peeled and cubed
Salt and pepper to taste
2 cups (500ml) vegetable stock
2 cups (500ml) grated Cheddar cheese (8 oz. / 225g)

Remove eggplant flesh with a spoon, leaving a 1/4-inch (6mm) layer next to skin. Sprinkle skins and flesh with salt and drain in separate colanders 20 minutes. Preheat oven to 400F (200C).

Heat oil in large skillet. Cook peppers, celery and onion over low heat about 15 minutes. Stir in rice and continue to cook gently. Roughly chop eggplant flesh and add to skillet. Add tomatoes, salt, pepper and vegetable stock. Cook over low heat about 15 minutes.

Place stuffing in eggplant skins, sprinkle with grated cheese and bake in oven 45 minutes.

Makes 6 servings.

Variation
Replace rice with bulgur wheat and reduce cooking times on stove and in oven.

Each serving contains:

Cal	Prot	Carb	Fib	Tot. Fat	Sat. Fat	Chol	Sodium
416	14g	38g	7g	25g	10g	40mg	308mg

Eggplant Parmigiana

This Italian dish is the favorite of many.

1 eggplant (1-1/2 to 2 lb. / 700-900g)
Salt
3 tablespoons (45ml) all-purpose flour
1-1/2 cups (375ml) dry breadcrumbs
2 eggs, beaten
Vegetable oil for frying
1 can (15-oz. / 425g) tomato sauce
1 tablespoon (15ml) tomato paste
1/4 cup (60ml) water
1 tablespoon (15ml) fresh basil leaves, or 1 teaspoon (5ml) dried
*   basil*
Salt and pepper to taste
12 oz. (340g) mozzarella cheese, sliced
1/2 cup (125ml) grated Parmesan cheese (2 oz. / 60g)

Preheat oven to 350F (175C). Lightly grease a shallow baking dish.

Slice eggplant crosswise into 1/2-inch (1.25cm) rounds. Sprinkle with salt. Combine flour and breadcrumbs in a shallow pan. Dip eggplant slices into beaten eggs, then into breadcrumb mixture. In a large skillet, heat oil and sauté both sides of eggplant until golden. Drain on paper towels.

Combine tomato sauce, tomato paste, water, basil, salt and pepper. Spoon 2 to 3 tablespoons (30-45ml) sauce into baking dish. Place a layer of eggplant over sauce, cover with a layer of mozzarella. Repeat layers, ending with cheese. Sprinkle with Parmesan cheese.

Bake 20 to 25 minutes, until cheese has melted and is golden brown. Serve at once.

Makes 6 servings.

Each serving contains:

Cal	Prot	Carb	Fib	Tot. Fat	Sat. Fat	Chol	Sodium
480	22g	39g	6g	27g	11g	122mg	1147mg

Pizza

Vegetable-topped pizza with a minimum of cheese makes a quick supper main dish. Add cooked sausage, if you wish. For an extra-quick pizza, use a prepared pizza crust.

Pizza dough:
1 pkg. (1/4-oz. / 8g) dry yeast
3/4 cup (185ml) warm water
2-1/2 cups (625ml) buttermilk baking mix
1 tablespoon (15ml) olive oil

1 small Japanese eggplant (1/2 lb. / 225g), cut crosswise into 1/4-inch (6mm) slices
1 can (8-1/2-oz. / 240g) artichoke hearts, drained
1/2 green bell pepper, chopped
2 tomatoes, sliced
1/2 cup (125ml) sliced olives
2 teaspoons (10ml) dried basil leaves
2 teaspoons (10ml) dried oregano leaves
2 teaspoons (10ml) chopped parsley
3-4 tablespoons (45-60ml) olive oil
1 cup (250ml) shredded Monterey Jack or crumbled feta cheese (4 oz. / 115g)

Dissolve yeast in warm water. Let stand 5 to 10 minutes, until bubbly. Stir into baking mix and oil. Knead 4 to 5 minutes, adding more baking mix if needed. Set aside and let dough rest 10 minutes.

Preheat oven to 425F (220C). Lightly grease 2 pizza pans or cookie sheets.

Divide dough in half. On a floured board, roll out each half to desired shape. Place on prepared pans. Arrange vegetables on top, sprinkle with herbs and drizzle with oil. Top with cheese. Bake 18 to 20 minutes, until golden brown.

Makes 4 servings.

Variations
1. Mix the herbs into the crust.

2. Use oil from the canned artichokes instead of olive oil.

Each serving contains:

Cal	Prot	Carb	Fib	Tot. Fat	Sat. Fat	Chol	Sodium
657	16g	63g	9g	39g	10g	26mg	1276mg

Vegetarian Moussaka

Bouquet garni is a combination of herbs used to add flavoring and discarded before serving. For easy removal, the herbs are tied in a bundle or placed in a cheesecloth bag.

> *1-1/2 lb. (700g) eggplant, cut crosswise into thin slices*
> *Salt*
> *1 onion, finely chopped*
> *Oil for sautéing*
> *3 tomatoes, peeled and cubed*
> *1/4 lb. (115g) fresh mushrooms, sliced*
> *6 celery ribs, finely chopped*
> *3 garlic cloves, crushed*
> *1 bouquet garni (bay leaf, thyme, parsley)*
> *Pepper to taste*
> *1-1/2 cups (375ml) rice*
> *2 cups (500ml) water*
> *3 eggs, beaten*
> *1 cup (250ml) sour cream*
> *1 cup (250ml) grated Gruyère or Parmesan cheese (4 oz. / 115g)*

Sprinkle eggplant slices with salt and drain in colander 20 minutes. Pat dry with paper towels.

Sauté onion gently in a little oil. When it begins to turn golden, add tomatoes, mushrooms, celery, garlic, bouquet garni, salt and pepper. Cook 30 minutes to reduce the liquid. Discard bouquet garni.

In a large skillet, heat oil and sauté eggplant slices on both sides until golden. Drain on paper towels or in a colander.

Preheat oven to 375F (190C). Grease a baking dish.

Pour rice into a saucepan over high heat. Stir vigorously for 1 minute with a wooden spoon. Pour in water, season with salt and reduce heat. Cook until water has evaporated. Add to tomato mixture. Combine eggs and sour cream.

In prepared dish, alternate layers of eggplant and tomato-rice mixture, finishing with eggplant. Top with sour-cream sauce and sprinkle with grated cheese. Bake 30 minutes. Serve hot.

Makes 6 servings.

Each serving contains:

Cal	Prot	Carb	Fib	Tot. Fat	Sat. Fat	Chol	Sodium
388	13g	27g	5g	26g	11g	143mg	209mg

Eggplant-Mushroom Stir-Fry

(Russia)

You may prefer to peel the eggplant before cutting it up, especially if the skin is thick.

> *3 tablespoons (45ml) olive oil or sunflower oil*
> *1 onion, chopped*
> *1-1/4 lb. (575g) button mushrooms, sliced*
> *1-1/2 lb. (700g) eggplant, cut into 1/2-inch (1.25cm) cubes*
> *1 green bell pepper, sliced*
> *3-4 tablespoons (45-60ml) vegetable stock or white wine*
> *1 tablespoon (15ml) chopped parsley*
> *1 tablespoon (15ml) dill weed*
> *Salt and pepper to taste*
> *Hot cooked rice*
> *Sour cream (optional)*
> *Toasted breadcrumbs for topping*

Heat 1 tablespoon (15ml) oil in wok or large skillet. Sauté onion and mushrooms about 5 minutes. Add remaining oil, eggplant and bell pepper. Stir-fry 3 to 4 minutes. Stir in stock or wine, reduce heat and simmer about 15 minutes, until vegetables are tender. Stir in parsley, dill, salt and pepper.

Serve over rice, topped with a dollop of sour cream, if using, and sprinkled with breadcrumbs.

Makes 6 servings.

Each serving contains:

Cal	Prot	Carb	Fib	Tot. Fat	Sat. Fat	Chol	Sodium
215	6g	33g	6g	8g	1g	0mg	93mg

Vegetarian Lasagna

Make sure the spinach is well drained before assembling the ingredients.

1-1/2 lb. (700g) eggplant, cut lengthwise into thin slices
Salt
Olive oil or sunflower oil for frying
5 tomatoes, peeled and cubed
3 garlic cloves, crushed
1 onion, chopped
Pepper to taste
2 teaspoons (10ml) Italian seasoning
1 pkg. (10-oz. / 280g) frozen spinach, thawed
1/2 lb. (225g) lasagna strips
1 cup (125ml) shredded mozzarella cheese (4 oz. / 115g)
Grated Gruyère or Parmesan cheese (optional)

Sprinkle eggplant slices with salt and drain in colander 20 minutes. Pat dry with paper towels. Preheat oven to 375F (190C). Lightly grease a large baking dish.

Heat a little oil in a saucepan and add tomatoes, garlic, onion, salt, pepper and Italian seasoning. Cover and cook over low heat about 15 minutes, stirring occasionally.

Heat oil in a skillet and sauté eggplant slices lightly on both sides. Drain in a colander or on paper towels. Squeeze excess water from thawed spinach.

Cook lasagna as directed on package. Drain.

Line prepared baking dish with lasagna strips. Alternate layers of eggplant, tomato mixture, spinach, mozzarella and lasagna, finishing with lasagna and sauce. Cover with grated cheese, if using.

Bake about 30 minutes.

Makes 6 servings.

Each serving contains:

Cal	Prot	Carb	Fib	Tot. Fat	Sat. Fat	Chol	Sodium
221	9g	28g	6g	10g	3g	15mg	164mg

Double-Curry Eggplant
(India)

If you like curry, you'll love this doubled-up version.

> *1-1/2 lb. (700g) eggplant, peeled and cubed*
> *Salt*
> *2 teaspoons (10ml) curry powder*
> *1/2 cup (125ml) water*
> *2 tablespoons (30ml) oil*
> *1 onion, finely chopped*
> *1/4 cup (60ml) raisins*
> *1 apple, peeled and chopped*
> *Cooked rice*
> *Curry Dressing, below*

Sprinkle eggplant cubes with salt and drain in colander 20 minutes. Pat dry with paper towels. Dissolve curry powder in water.

Heat oil in a large pan and sauté onion gently. Add curry liquid, eggplant, raisins and apple. Cook 1 minute over high heat, stirring constantly. Cover and simmer until eggplant is tender, about 20 minutes. Stir occasionally, adding a little oil if mixture starts to stick.

Serve over rice, topped with Curry Dressing.

Makes 6 servings.

Each serving contains:

Cal	Prot	Carb	Fib	Tot. Fat	Sat. Fat	Chol	Sodium
289	5g	35g	6g	15g	3g	9mg	121mg

Curry Dressing

3/4 cup (185ml) plain yogurt
1/4 cup (60ml) mayonnaise
1-2 teaspoons (5-10ml) curry powder
1-2 tablespoons (15-30ml) lemon or lime juice
2 tablespoons (30ml) chopped peanuts
1 tablespoon (15ml) chopped chives

Combine all ingredients. Mix well.

Makes 1 cup (250ml).

One serving contains:

Cal	Prot	Carb	Fib	Tot. Fat	Sat. Fat	Chol	Sodium
106	2g	3g	0g	10g	2g	10mg	67mg

Eggplant Tempura

(Japan)

It is important to use ice-cold water in the batter. This aids the puffing and appearance of the coating.

1 egg white
1-1/4 cups (310ml) ice water
1/4 cup (60ml) cornstarch
1 cup (250ml) all-purpose flour
1/2 teaspoon (2ml) baking powder
Oil for frying
2 small Japanese eggplants, each 1/4 lb. (115g), cut diagonally
*   into 1/4-inch (6mm) slices*
2 green bell peppers, cut into strips
2 sweet potatoes, peeled and thinly sliced
Cooked rice
Tempura Sauce, below

In a small bowl, beat egg white until frothy. Stir in water until well blended. Combine cornstarch, flour and baking powder. Pour egg mixture into dry ingredients. Stir briefly; batter should be lumpy. Place batter bowl in a larger bowl of ice water to keep batter cold.

Heat oil in a deep fryer (350F / 175C) or deep saucepan. Dip vegetables into batter, shake to remove excess and lower into oil. Cook until golden, remove and drain on paper towels.

Serve with rice, offering the sauce as a dip for vegetables.

Makes 6 servings.

Each serving contains:

Cal	Prot	Carb	Fib	Tot. Fat	Sat. Fat	Chol	Sodium
320	7g	50g	4g	10g	1g	0mg	532mg

Tempura Sauce

2 tablespoons (30ml) soy sauce
1/4 cup (60ml) dashi or chicken broth
2 tablespoons (30ml) mirin or cream sherry
1 tablespoon (15ml) grated fresh ginger

Combine all ingredients.

Makes 1/2 cup (125ml).

One serving contains:

Cal	Prot	Carb	Fib	Tot. Fat	Sat. Fat	Chol	Sodium
13	1g	1g	0g	0g	0g	0mg	471mg

Chickpea Stew

Barraniya
("Pied-Noir" Cuisine)

Chickpeas, also known as *garbanzo beans,* were first cultivated in the Middle East, but are now available—and popular—worldwide. They are a good source of protein and fiber.

> *1-1/4 lb. (310g) eggplant, cut into 1-inch (2.5cm) cubes*
> *Salt*
> *3 tablespoons (45ml) oil*
> *2 garlic cloves, chopped*
> *1-2 jalapeño peppers, seeded and chopped*
> *1 teaspoon (5ml) ground cumin*
> *1 teaspoon (5ml) mild chili powder*
> *1 teaspoon (5ml) dried oregano*
> *1 can (15-oz. / 425g) chickpeas or garbanzo beans, undrained*
> *1 pkg. (10-oz. / 280g) frozen mixed vegetables, thawed*
> *1/2 cup (125ml) peas*
> *2 tablespoons (30ml) tomato paste*
> *2 cups (500ml) Béchamel Sauce, page 161*
> *Fresh chopped chives for topping*

Sprinkle eggplant with salt and drain in colander 20 minutes. Pat dry with paper towels. Place in a saucepan with water to cover and boil 5 to 7 minutes. Drain. Preheat oven to 350F (175C).

Heat oil in large skillet and sauté garlic and jalapeños. Stir in cumin, chili powder and oregano. Add eggplant and other vegetables and mix thoroughly. Add salt and pepper to taste.

Spoon mixture into shallow baking dish. Stir tomato paste into béchamel sauce and pour over eggplant mixture. Sprinkle with chives. Bake 15 to 20 minutes.

Makes 6 servings.

Each serving contains:

Cal	Prot	Carb	Fib	Tot. Fat	Sat. Fat	Chol	Sodium
327	9g	36g	10g	18g	7g	27mg	380mg

Layered Stove-Top Casserole
Ailazan
(Armenia)

Here eggplant is combined with two of its close relatives—potatoes and tomatoes. All are members of the nightshade family.

1-1/2 lb. (700g) eggplant, peeled
Salt
4 potatoes, peeled and cubed
1 green bell pepper, cut into thin strips
1 red bell pepper, cut into thin strips
1 yellow bell pepper, cut into thin strips
1 onion, roughly chopped
5 oz. (145g) green beans, cut into 1-inch (2.5cm) pieces
2 tomatoes, peeled and cubed
1 tablespoon (15ml) chopped basil
1 tablespoon (15ml) chopped marjoram
Sunflower oil to taste
1/2 cup (125ml) water
Pepper to taste

Cut eggplant crosswise into 1/2-inch (1.25cm) slices. Sprinkle with salt and drain in colander 20 minutes. Pat dry with paper towels.

In a Dutch oven or heavy saucepan, alternate layers of eggplant, potatoes, peppers, onion, beans and tomatoes. Add basil and marjoram. Sprinkle with oil and add water.

Season with salt and pepper to taste. Cover with a plate pressed down on the vegetables and then with the pan lid. Cook over low heat about 30 minutes.

Makes 6 servings.

Each serving contains:

Cal	Prot	Carb	Fib	Tot. Fat	Sat. Fat	Chol	Sodium
227	4g	34g	6g	10g	1g	0mg	61mg

Eggplant and Pasta

Artichokes packed in oil add more flavor than those that are water-packed or frozen.

> *1-1/2 lb. (700g) eggplant, peeled*
> *Salt*
> *2 onions, finely chopped*
> *Oil for sautéing*
> *Cooked pasta shells*
> *1 bottle (10-oz. / 280g) artichoke hearts, drained and sliced*
> *2 tablespoons (30ml) chopped red bell pepper*
> *3 tablespoons (45ml) cashews*
> *1/2 teaspoon (2ml) fennel seeds*
> *1 tablespoon (15ml) chopped parsley*
> *2-3 green onions*
> *3 tomatoes, chopped*
> *Grated Parmesan cheese for garnish*

Cut eggplant into strips (1 x 4-inch / 2.5x10cm) strips. Sprinkle with salt and drain in colander 20 minutes. Heat saucepan of water and boil eggplant 5 to 7 minutes. Drain and pat dry with paper towels. Preheat oven to 425F (220C). Gently sauté onions in hot oil until transparent.

In a baking dish, layer pasta, eggplant, onion, artichokes, bell pepper and salt to taste. Sprinkle with cashews, fennel seeds, parsley, green onions and tomatoes. Bake about 15 minutes, until heated through. Top with Parmesan cheese.

Makes 6 servings.

Each serving contains:

Cal	Prot	Carb	Fib	Tot. Fat	Sat. Fat	Chol	Sodium
285	10g	43g	6g	9g	2g	3mg	298mg

Main Dishes with Meat

The gorgeous purple shell of an eggplant is a natural container for a stuffing. Previous chapters have provided several vegetable stuffings. Here, now, are meat combinations you will love— Stuffed Eggplant Casserole, with ground meat and spices; Ham-Filled Eggplants; Italian Baked Eggplants with Sausage; and Stuffed Eggplants from Provence, with ground beef, mushrooms and olives.

Moussaka, a favorite throughout the Middle East, is given in oven and stove-top versions. From Provence come two beef stews, and from Morocco a lamb stew known as *Tajine*. China provides a Pork Stir-Fry, which is not surprising, but would you have thought to include eggplant?

Lamb is featured in Lamb Kebabs and Stuffed Eggplant Fans. And, of course, there is chicken— from Provence, Turkey and Armenia.

Eggplant is not the main ingredient in these dishes, but it adds flavor and texture and definitely makes its presence known.

Stuffed Eggplant Casserole

The spicy filling will have everyone reaching for seconds.

> *2-3 tablespoons (30-45ml) sesame seeds*
> *2 eggplants, each 1 lb. (450g), cut in half lengthwise*
> *Salt*
> *3/4 lb. (340g) ground beef, pork or lamb*
> *1 onion, chopped*
> *1/4 teaspoon (1ml) ground ginger*
> *1/4 teaspoon (1ml) ground cinnamon*
> *1/4 teaspoon (1ml) ground nutmeg*
> *1/4 teaspoon (1ml) garlic powder*
> *Pepper to taste*
> *1 cup (250ml) cooked rice*
> *2 tomatoes, peeled and chopped*
> *3 tablespoons (45ml) breadcrumbs*
> *2 tablespoons (30ml) chopped cilantro*

Preheat oven to 425F (200C). Oil a baking pan. Toast sesame seeds by heating in a dry skillet 1 to 2 minutes.

Make several slashes in eggplant flesh. Sprinkle with salt. Place cut side up prepared baking pan. Bake 25 to 30 minutes until tender. Remove and let cool 5 minutes. Remove flesh with a spoon, leaving a 1/4-inch (6mm) layer next to skin. Chop eggplant flesh.

In a skillet, brown meat and onion. Add ginger, cinnamon, nutmeg, garlic powder, salt and pepper. Add rice and tomatoes and mix well. Spoon mixture into eggplant shells.

Combine breadcrumbs, sesame seeds and cilantro. Sprinkle over eggplant stuffing. Return to oven and bake 15 to 20 minutes until heated.

Makes 6 servings.

Each serving contains:

Cal	Prot	Carb	Fib	Tot. Fat	Sat. Fat	Chol	Sodium
241	15g	25g	6g	10g	4g	39mg	117mg

Mixed Vegetable and Beef Gratin

Serve pilaf as an accompaniment to this dish.

1-1/2 lb. (700g) eggplant, peeled
Salt
1 lb. (450g) ground beef
1 onion, chopped
1 green bell pepper, sliced
1 celery rib, sliced
1 carrot, peeled and sliced
2 garlic cloves, minced
2 tomatoes, peeled and chopped
1 cup (250ml) water or white wine
1 bouquet garni (bay leaf, thyme, parsley)
Pepper
1/2 cup (125ml) breadcrumbs
2 tablespoons (30ml) chopped chives
1/2 cup (125ml) shredded Gruyère cheese (2 oz. / 60g)

Cut eggplant into sticks (1 x 2-inch / 2.5x5cm). Sprinkle with salt and drain in colander 20 minutes. Pat dry with paper towels.

Brown beef in a large skillet. Stir in onion, bell pepper, celery, carrot, garlic and tomatoes. Add water or wine and bouquet garni. Reduce heat, cover and simmer about 20 minutes. Discard bouquet garni.

Preheat oven to 350F (175C). Spoon mixture into a gratin pan or baking dish. Mix in eggplant and salt and pepper to taste. Combine breadcrumbs, chives and cheese and sprinkle over mixture. Bake, uncovered, 20 minutes or until top is golden.

Makes 6 servings.

Each serving contains:

Cal	Prot	Carb	Fib	Tot. Fat	Sat. Fat	Chol	Sodium
257	21g	20g	5g	11g	5g	37mg	220mg

Armenian Meatballs and Eggplant
Duezmeh

Everyone will love this unusual treatment of meatballs.

1-1/2 lb. (700g) eggplant, cut into cubes
Salt
1 lb. (450g) ground beef
1/2 lb. (225g) ground pork or lamb
1 onion, chopped
1 egg, beaten
2 tablespoons (30ml) chopped parsley
Pepper to taste
2 tablespoons (30ml) oil
3 tomatoes, sliced
3 green bell peppers, sliced into strips
Tomato Sauce, below

Sprinkle eggplant with salt and drain in colander 20 minutes. Pat dry with paper towels.

Combine meats, onion, egg, parsley and salt and pepper to taste. Shape into small flattened meatballs and lightly brown in oil. Set aside on paper towels.

Preheat oven to 375F (190C). In a baking dish alternate layers of eggplant and meatballs. Cover with tomato slices and pepper strips. Pour tomato sauce over all. Bake 30 minutes.

Makes 6 servings.

Each serving contains:

Cal	Prot	Carb	Fib	Tot. Fat	Sat. Fat	Chol	Sodium
388	27g	25g	7g	21g	6g	88mg	417mg

Tomato Sauce

1 onion, chopped
1 tablespoon (15ml) oil
1 lb. (450g) tomatoes
1 can (6-oz. / 170g) tomato paste
1 cup (250g) water
Salt and pepper to taste

Sauté onion in oil until soft. Add remaining ingredients and cook to desired consistency.

Makes 2-1/2 cups.

One serving contains:

Cal	Prot	Carb	Fib	Tot. Fat	Sat. Fat	Chol	Sodium
66	2g	10g	2g	3g	0g	0mg	277mg

Moussaka

(Greece, Turkey, Romania)

Vary this versatile dish as much as you choose. Use a different combination of meat and vegetables each time you make it.

1-1/2 lb. (700g) eggplant, cut crosswise into 1/4-inch (6mm) slices
Salt
2 tablespoons (30ml) butter
1 onion, chopped
1 lb. (450g) ground beef or lamb
1 cup (250ml) water
3 tomatoes, peeled and chopped
2 tablespoons (30ml) chopped parsley
3 garlic cloves, chopped
1/4 lb. (115g) fresh mushrooms, sliced
Pepper to taste
1/3 cup (80ml) white wine
2 eggs, separated
1/2 cup (125ml) breadcrumbs
Oil for frying
1 cup (250ml) Béchamel Sauce, page 161
1/2 cup (125ml) grated Gruyère cheese (2 oz. / 60g)

Sprinkle eggplant slices with salt and drain in colander 20 minutes. Pat dry with paper towels.

Melt butter in a skillet and sauté onion gently. Add meat and water. Stir meat well during the cooking, breaking up any lumps. Add tomatoes, parsley, garlic and mushrooms. Mix well, season with salt and pepper and pour in wine. Cover and simmer 45 minutes over low heat, stirring occasionally.

Preheat oven to 400F (200C). Beat egg whites until stiff.

When meat mixture is cooked, add 3 tablespoons (45ml) bread-crumbs and beaten egg whites.

Fry eggplant slices quickly in oil until golden. Set aside on paper towels to drain.

Sprinkle remaining breadcrumbs in a greased dish. Alternate layers of eggplant slices and meat sauce, finishing with eggplant.

Beat egg yolks and add to béchamel sauce; add half the cheese. Pour sauce over eggplant and sprinkle remaining grated cheese on top.

Bake in oven 45 minutes. Serve hot.

Makes 6 servings.

Each serving contains:

Cal	Prot	Carb	Fib	Tot. Fat	Sat. Fat	Chol	Sodium
472	25g	24g	5g	30g	12g	134mg	333mg

Armenian Beef and Walnuts
Kharjana

Eggs bind everything together and walnuts provide the crunch in this flavorful Armenian-style hash.

1 lb. (450g) eggplant, peeled and grated
Salt
3/4 lb. (340g) ground beef
1 onion, chopped
1 tablespoon (15ml) oil
2 tablespoons (30ml) butter
1/2 cup (125ml) chopped walnuts
2 tablespoons (30ml) chopped parsley
2 tablespoons (30ml) chopped pimento
Pepper to taste
4 eggs
Shredded Cheddar cheese (optional)

Sprinkle eggplant with salt and drain in colander 20 minutes. Pat dry with paper towels.

Brown meat in a large skillet. Add oil and butter and sauté onion.

In a bowl combine eggplant, walnuts, parsley, pimento and salt and pepper to taste. Stir into meat and cook, stirring, about 10 minutes. Add eggs and mix well. Cover and cook about 3 minutes. Stir mixture and sprinkle top with cheese, if using. Cover and continue cooking until eggs are set. Or place skillet under a broiler after adding cheese and broil until cheese is lightly browned.

Makes 6 servings.

Each serving contains:

Cal	Prot	Carb	Fib	Tot. Fat	Sat. Fat	Chol	Sodium
292	19g	9g	3g	21g	6g	173mg	171mg

Stove-Top Moussaka

(Arab Cuisine)

This is less rich than the traditional moussaka—perfect for summer, when you want to eat lightly and avoid using the oven.

1-1/2 lb. (700g) eggplant, cut into 1-inch (2.5cm) cubes
Salt
2 tablespoons (30ml) butter
1 onion, chopped
1 lb. (450g) ground beef
1 cup (250ml) water
3 tomatoes, peeled and chopped
2 tablespoons (30ml) chopped parsley
3 garlic cloves, chopped
1/4 lb. (115g) fresh mushrooms sliced
1/2 cup (125ml) sliced carrots
1 bell pepper, sliced
Pepper to taste
1/3 cup (80ml) white wine
1 pkg. (10 oz. / 280g) frozen spinach, mixed vegetables
   or asparagus.
1/2 cup (125ml) breadcrumbs
1/2 cup (125ml) grated Gruyère cheese (2 oz. / 60g)

Sprinkle eggplant cubes with salt and drain in colander 20 minutes. Pat dry with paper towels.

Melt butter in a large saucepan or Dutch oven and sauté onion gently. Add ground beef and water. Stir meat well during the cooking, breaking up any lumps. Add tomatoes, eggplant, parsley, garlic, mushrooms, carrots and bell pepper. Mix well, season with salt and pepper and pour in wine. Cover and simmer 30 minutes over low heat, stirring occasionally and adding water as needed. Add spinach, mixed vegetables or asparagus and cook 10 minutes. Top with breadcrumbs and grated cheese.

Makes 6 servings.

Each serving contains:

Cal	Prot	Carb	Fib	Tot. Fat	Sat. Fat	Chol	Sodium
320	23g	24g	6g	15g	7g	48mg	297mg

Meat and Spinach Bake

Be careful with the cinnamon. A little bit goes a long way.

1 lb. (450g) eggplant, cut lengthwise into 1/2-inch (1.25cm) slices
Salt
1/2 lb. (225g) ground beef
1/2 lb. (225g) pork sausage
1 onion, chopped
3 sun-dried tomatoes, drained and chopped
1 can (8-oz. / 225g) tomato sauce
1/8-1/4 teaspoon (1/2-1ml) cinnamon
Dash of nutmeg
Salt and pepper to taste
2 pkg. (10-oz. / 280g) frozen spinach, thawed and drained
1 cup (250ml) plain yogurt
Grated Parmesan cheese for topping

Sprinkle eggplant slices with salt and drain in colander 20 minutes. Pat dry with paper towels.

In a skillet, brown beef and sausage, stirring often. Drain excess fat. Add onion, tomatoes, tomato sauce, cinnamon, nutmeg, salt and pepper. Preheat broiler.

Brush eggplant slices with oil and broil 3 to 4 minutes on each side. Reduce oven temperature to 350F (175C).

In a baking dish, alternate layers of eggplant, meat mixture, spinach and dollops of yogurt. Sprinkle top with Parmesan. Bake about 45 minutes.

Makes 6 servings.

Each serving contains:

Cal	Prot	Carb	Fib	Tot. Fat	Sat. Fat	Chol	Sodium
314	23g	16g	6g	19g	7g	54mg	1007mg

Hungarian Beef and Eggplant

Here are traditional Hungarian flavors enhanced by the addition of eggplant.

1 lb. (450g) small Japanese eggplants, cut diagonally
into 1/2-inch (1.25cm) slices
Salt
1 lb. (450g) flank steak, thinly sliced in 2-inch (5cm) strips
3 tablespoons (45ml) oil
1 onion, sliced
1 green bell pepper, cut into strips
1 jalapeño pepper, seeded and chopped
1 tablespoon (15ml) paprika
2 teaspoons (5ml) sugar
1 can (14-1/2 oz.) (411g) tomatoes, with juice
Pepper to taste
Sour cream for garnish
Dill weed for garnish

Sprinkle eggplant with salt and drain in colander 20 minutes. Pat dry with paper towels.

In a large skillet, brown steak in hot oil. Add onion, peppers, eggplant and paprika. Reduce heat and simmer 10 minutes. Stir in sugar and tomatoes and cook 15 minutes longer. Season with salt and pepper to taste. Serve with a dollop of sour cream and a sprinkle of dill weed.

Makes 6 servings.

Each serving contains:

Cal	Prot	Carb	Fib	Tot. Fat	Sat. Fat	Chol	Sodium
278	18g	14g	3g	17g	6g	48mg	215mg

Beef Stew from Provence

Boeuf aux Aubergines

This beef stew is fancy enough for company.

> *1 lb. (450g) eggplant, cut crosswise into 1/2-inch (1cm) slices*
> *Salt*
> *2 lb. (900g) beef stew meat, cut into 1-inch (2.5cm) cubes*
> *All-purpose flour for coating*
> *4 tablespoons (60ml) olive oil*
> *4 tablespoons (60ml) butter*
> *4 garlic cloves, crushed*
> *1 cup (250ml) white wine*
> *Pepper to taste*
> *Bouquet garni (bay leaf, thyme, parsley)*
> *1 lb. (450g) tomatoes, peeled and chopped*
> *1/2 lb. (225g) whole button mushrooms*
> *1/2 cup (125ml) black olives*
> *Chopped fresh parsley for garnish*

Sprinkle eggplant with salt and drain in colander 20 minutes. Pat dry with paper towels. Dredge meat cubes in flour

In a large saucepan, heat 1 tablespoon (15ml) olive oil and butter. Fry meat quickly, turning occasionally, until brown on all sides. Add garlic, wine, salt, pepper and bouquet garni. Cook 10 minutes, uncovered, over high heat, to reduce liquid. Cover, reduce heat and cook 45 minutes.

When meat is cooked, add tomatoes, mushrooms and olives. Cook, uncovered, 5 minutes. Discard bouquet garni.

Heat remaining oil in a skillet and sauté eggplant slices. Drain; sprinkle with salt.

Turn meat onto platter and surround with eggplant slices. Garnish with parsley.

Makes 6 servings.

Each serving contains:

Cal	Prot	Carb	Fib	Tot. Fat	Sat. Fat	Chol	Sodium
531	29g	16g	4g	37g	14g	113mg	460mg

Haitian-Style Stew

Aubergines aux Deux Viandes

This tangy stew is even better the second day.

1 lb. (450g) beef stew meat, cut into 1/2-inch (1.25cm) cubes
1/4 lb. (115g) bacon or salt pork, cubed
1/2 teaspoon paprika
1 onion, sliced
1 red bell pepper, sliced
1 fresh green chile pepper, sliced
1 tablespoon (15ml) chopped cilantro
1/2 cup (125ml) water
1 lb. (450g) eggplant, cut into cubes
Salt
1 tablespoon (15ml) capers
1 pkg. (10-oz. / 280g) frozen peas
1 cup (250ml) cooked kernel corn
1/4 cup (60ml) oil
1/4 cup (60ml) vinegar
Pepper to taste

In a Dutch oven or heavy pan, brown all sides of beef and bacon or salt pork. Sprinkle with paprika and stir to coat. Stir in onion, peppers and cilantro. Add water, cover and reduce heat. Simmer about 1 hour until tender.

Sprinkle eggplant cubes with salt and drain in colander 20 minutes. Pat dry with paper towels.

Add eggplant and capers to meat mixture. Cover and cook until eggplant is tender. Add peas and corn and heat through. Combine oil and vinegar and stir into mixture. Add salt and pepper to taste.

Makes 6 servings.

Each serving contains:

Cal	Prot	Carb	Fib	Tot. Fat	Sat. Fat	Chol	Sodium
352	19g	21g	6g	22g	6g	51mg	554mg

Eggplant Ragoût

The French word *ragoûter* means "to stimulate the appetite." This stew will both stimulate and satisfy.

> *1 lb. (450g) Japanese eggplant*
> *Salt*
> *2 tablespoons (30ml) oil*
> *1 lb. (450g) beef-stew meat, cut into 1/2-inch (1.25cm) cubes*
> *All-purpose flour for coating*
> *1 large onion, sliced*
> *2 garlic cloves, crushed*
> *2 carrots, thinly sliced*
> *1 celery rib, sliced*
> *1-3/4 to 2 cups (440-500ml) tomato juice*
> *1 beef bouillon cube*
> *2 teaspoons (10ml) paprika*
> *Pepper to taste*
> *2 tablespoons (30ml) chopped parsley*

Cut eggplant crosswise into 1/2-inch (1.25cm) slices and cut each slice into sixths. Sprinkle with salt and drain in colander 20 minutes. Pat dry with paper towels.

Heat oil in Dutch oven or large saucepan. Toss beef in flour to coat, shake off excess flour and brown beef in oil. Add onion, garlic, carrots and celery and stir briefly. Add tomato juice, bouillon cube and paprika. Cover and cook about 25 minutes.

Add eggplant. Cover and cook about 30 minutes longer. Season with salt and pepper and garnish with parsley.

Makes 6 servings.

Each serving contains:

Cal	Prot	Carb	Fib	Tot. Fat	Sat. Fat	Chol	Sodium
257	16g	17g	4g	14g	4g	46mg	643mg

Lamb Chops with Eggplant

Missou Kaladjoche
(Armenia)

Lamb is a symbol of hospitality throughout the Middle East, where it is served to honor special guests.

> *1 lb. (450g) eggplant, cut into large cubes*
> *2 onions, chopped*
> *1 celery rib, chopped*
> *1 carrot, shredded*
> *Oil to taste*
> *6 lamb chops or cutlets*
> *Salt and pepper to taste*
> *Fresh thyme to taste*
> *1 cup (250ml) Tomato Sauce, page 119*

Soak eggplant cubes in salted water 20 minutes. Drain and pat dry with paper towels. Preheat oven to 400F (200C).

Place onions, celery and carrot in a baking dish. Cover with eggplant cubes and pour over a little oil. Bake 30 minutes.

Season chops or cutlets with salt and pepper and sprinkle generously with thyme. Place on top of the eggplant and return to oven. Turn meat over after 8 minutes and remove from oven when cooked.

Heat tomato sauce and pour over the meat to serve. Serve very hot.

Makes 6 servings.

Each serving contains:

Cal	Prot	Carb	Fib	Tot. Fat	Sat. Fat	Chol	Sodium
314	18g	15g	4g	21g	7g	64mg	219mg

Lamb Kebabs

Chopkebab

(Armenia)

Try this for your next cookout. It's sure to be a winner.

Marinade:
3/4 cup (185ml) olive oil
1/2 cup (125ml) lemon juice
3 garlic cloves, minced
1 tablespoon (15ml) dried oregano leaves
1 tablespoon (15ml) ground turmeric
Salt and pepper to taste

1-3/4 lb. (800g) boneless lamb, cut into 1-inch (2.5cm) cubes
1 lb. (450g) eggplant, cut into 1-inch (2.5cm) cubes
18 small mushroom caps
18 cherry tomatoes
2 green bell peppers, cut into 1-inch (2.5cm) squares
Cooked brown rice

Thoroughly combine oil, lemon juice, garlic, oregano, turmeric, salt and pepper in a bowl. Add lamb cubes. Cover and refrigerate 3 to 4 hours. Preheat grill or broiler. Remove lamb from marinade.

Toss eggplant cubes in marinade to coat. Thread alternating pieces of lamb, eggplant, mushrooms, tomatoes and bell peppers on skewers. Grill or broil, brushing with marinade. Turn often to brown all sides. Serve over rice.

Makes 6 servings.

Each serving contains:

Cal	Prot	Carb	Fib	Tot. Fat	Sat. Fat	Chol	Sodium
625	25g	30g	5g	46g	11g	83mg	118mg

131

Lamb in Tomato-Wine Sauce

Patlijan Hunkar Bayendi
(Armenia)

Vegetable cooking-oil spray is a handy alternative to brushing on oil.

> *2 tablespoons (30ml) oil*
> *1 lb. (450g) boneless lamb, cut into 1-inch (2.5cm) cubes*
> *2 onions, chopped*
> *1 teaspoon (5ml) salt*
> *1/2 teaspoon (2ml) pepper*
> *1/2 teaspoon (2ml) paprika*
> *6 oz. (170g) tomato paste*
> *1/2 cup (125ml) water*
> *1/2 cup (125ml) red wine*
> *1 lb. (450g) eggplant, cut into sticks (2 x 1/2-inch / 5x1.25cm)*
> *Parsley for garnish*

In a large saucepan, heat oil and cook lamb cubes until brown. Remove lamb and set aside. Fry onions gently in oil remaining in pan, then return lamb to pan. Season with salt and pepper and sprinkle with paprika. Mix together, cover and cook over high heat 5 minutes. Reduce heat, add tomato paste and water and continue cooking over low heat. After 30 minutes, add wine and cook another 15 minutes.

Lightly brush or spray eggplant with oil. Bake or broil until tender. Serve lamb over eggplant and sprinkle with chopped parsley.

Makes 6 servings.

Each serving contains:

Cal	Prot	Carb	Fib	Tot. Fat	Sat. Fat	Chol	Sodium
259	24g	14g	4g	11g	3g	67mg	636mg

Moroccan Tajine
Tajine d'Aubergines

Tajine is a Moroccan stew or an earthen casserole.

> *3 tablespoons (45ml) oil*
> *1 tablespoon (15ml) butter*
> *2 lb. (900g) lamb stew meat, cut into 1/2-inch (1.25cm) cubes*
> *1 onion, chopped*
> *1 garlic clove, minced*
> *2 carrots, peeled and sliced*
> *1 red bell pepper, sliced*
> *1-1/2 teaspoons (7ml) cumin*
> *Dash nutmeg*
> *1/2 teaspoon (2ml) ground ginger*
> *Dash cayenne pepper*
> *Saffron threads (optional)*
> *Salt and pepper to taste*
> *1 cup (250ml) white wine or water*
> *1 lb. (450g) eggplant, cut crosswise into 1/4-inch (6mm) slices*
> *Cooked couscous*

In a Dutch oven or tajine dish, heat oil and butter. Add lamb and brown all sides. Add onion and garlic, stir until softened. Add carrots, bell pepper and seasonings. Stir in wine or water. Reduce heat, cover and cook about 45 minutes.

Sprinkle eggplant with salt and drain in colander 20 minutes. Pat dry with paper towels.

Lightly brush or spray eggplant with oil. Broil slices 3 to 5 minutes on each side, until golden. To serve, line a platter with hot couscous, top with a layer of eggplant slices. Spoon meat over top.

Makes 6 servings.

Each serving contains:

Cal	Prot	Carb	Fib	Tot. Fat	Sat. Fat	Chol	Sodium
495	29g	24g	4g	28g	10g	97mg	351mg

Stuffed Eggplant Fans

Patlijan Karni Yarek

(Armenia)

Impress guests with this dish.

6 small Japanese eggplant (1 lb. / 450g)
Salt
2 tablespoons (30ml) butter, melted
2 tablespoons (30ml) oil
3/4 lb. (340g) ground lamb or beef
1 onion, chopped
1 green bell pepper, cut into strips
2 tomatoes, peeled and chopped
2 tablespoons (30ml) chopped pine nuts
1/4 teaspoon (1ml) ground allspice
1/4 teaspoon (1ml) ground cinnamon
2 tablespoons (30ml) chopped parsley
Pepper to taste

Cut each eggplant lengthwise into 1/4-inch (6mm) slices, without cutting through the stem, making a fan. Soak in salted water for 30 minutes. Remove from water and carefully pat dry without breaking fans. Preheat oven to 375F (190C).

Lightly brush fans with melted butter and place on a baking sheet. Bake about 20 minutes until golden.

Heat oil in a skillet and brown meat. Add onion, bell pepper, tomatoes, pine nuts, allspice, cinnamon, parsley and salt and pepper to taste. Stir and cook over low heat 15 minutes.

Place meat stuffing between "blades" of eggplant fans. Return to oven and bake 25 minutes.

Makes 6 servings.

Each serving contains:

Cal	Prot	Carb	Fib	Tot. Fat	Sat. Fat	Chol	Sodium
248	12g	10g	3g	19g	7g	48mg	122mg

Baked Tunisian Lamb and Eggplant

Aubergines au Mouton et à la Tomate

Cooked leftover beef or pork can be used as a substitute for the lamb.
Or use a combination of meats.

> *1-1/2 lb. (700g) Japanese eggplant, peeled and cut lengthwise into*
>   *thin slices*
> *Salt*
> *2 tablespoons (30ml) oil*
> *1/2 lb. (225g) cooked lamb or beef, chopped*
> *1 onion, chopped*
> *2 tomatoes, peeled and chopped*
> *1 teaspoon (5ml) dried oregano leaves*
> *1 teaspoon (5ml) dried rosemary leaves*
> *Pepper to taste*
> *1 cup (250ml) Tomato Sauce, page 119*

Sprinkle eggplant with salt and drain in colander 20 minutes. Pat dry
with paper towels.

In a large pan, heat oil and cook meat, onion and tomatoes, mixing
well. Add herbs and season with salt and pepper. Cook 15 minutes
over low heat, stirring occasionally.

Preheat oven to 375F (190C). Grease a baking dish. Alternate layers
of eggplant and meat in the dish, beginning and ending with eggplant. Pour tomato sauce over the top and bake 1 hour.

Makes 6 servings.

Each serving contains:

Cal	Prot	Carb	Fib	Tot. Fat	Sat. Fat	Chol	Sodium
187	13g	15g	5g	9g	2g	34mg	189mg

Greek-Style Stuffed Tomatoes

Melitzanes Yemistes

Make this dish when large ripe tomatoes are plentiful. Serve with a traditional Greek salad.

> *1 cup (250ml) shredded peeled eggplant (1 small)*
> *Salt*
> *8 large tomatoes*
> *1/2 lb. (225g) ground lamb or beef*
> *1 onion, chopped*
> *1 garlic clove, chopped*
> *1 carrot, shredded*
> *1 tablespoon (15ml) dried oregano leaves*
> *1 can (8-oz. / 225g) tomato sauce*
> *1/2 cup (125ml) uncooked couscous or rice*
> *1 cup (250ml) water*
> *1/4 cup (60ml) pine nuts*
> *1/4 cup (60ml) red wine*
> *Pepper*
> *3 tablespoons (45ml) olive oil*
> *4 oz. (115g) feta cheese, crumbled*

Sprinkle eggplant with salt and drain in colander 20 minutes. Pat dry with paper towels. Cut off tops of tomatoes, scoop out pulp and chop. Place tomato shells, cut side down, on paper towels to drain. Preheat oven to 350F (175C).

In a skillet brown meat. Add onion, garlic, carrot and oregano and sauté 2 to 3 minutes. Mix in chopped tomato, tomato sauce, rice, 1/2 cup (125ml) water, pine nuts, wine and salt and pepper to taste. Simmer about 20 minutes.

Place tomato shells in a baking dish. Layer meat mixture and cheese in shells, ending with cheese. Drizzle with olive oil. Pour remaining water into pan and bake 30 minutes, basting occasionally. Serve either hot or cold.

Makes 8 servings.

Each serving contains:

Cal	Prot	Carb	Fib	Tot. Fat	Sat. Fat	Chol	Sodium
287	12g	26g	4g	16g	5g	31mg	402mg

Pork Stir-Fry

(China)

Have all the ingredients ready before you start cooking. This one cooks in a hurry.

> *5 large dried Chinese mushrooms*
> *1 lb. (450g) Japanese eggplant, cut diagonally into 1/4-inch*
>   *(6mm) slices*
> *Salt*
> *2 tablespoons (30ml) oil*
> *2 garlic cloves, chopped*
> *1 tablespoon (15ml) grated fresh ginger*
> *1 green onion, sliced*
> *1/2 lb. (225g) boneless pork steak, thinly sliced*
> *1 pkg. (10-oz. / 280g) frozen broccoli spears, thawed*
> *1 teaspoon (5ml) cornstarch*
> *1/2 teaspoon (2ml) sugar*
> *2 tablespoons (30ml) vinegar*
> *3 tablespoons (45ml) soy sauce*
> *Pepper to taste*
> *1 teaspoon (5ml) sesame oil (optional)*
> *Cooked rice*

Soak mushrooms in a bowl of hot water for 15 minutes. Sprinkle eggplant with salt and drain in colander 20 minutes. Pat dry with paper towels. Cut broccoli stalks into 1-inch (2.5cm) pieces.

In a wok or deep skillet heat oil, add garlic, ginger and green onion. Cook about 30 seconds.

Add eggplant and stir-fry 3 to 4 minutes. Add pork and stir-fry until meat is browned. Add broccoli. Stir-fry 5 minutes, cover and cook until broccoli is tender-crisp.

In a small bowl dissolve cornstarch and sugar in vinegar and soy sauce. Pour over mixture in wok. Stir-fry until sauce thickens slightly. Stir in sesame oil, if using. Season with salt and pepper to taste. Serve over hot rice.

Makes 6 servings.

Each serving contains:

Cal	Prot	Carb	Fib	Tot. Fat	Sat. Fat	Chol	Sodium
263	15g	32g	4g	9g	2g	32mg	743mg

Grilled Eggplant Sandwich

A warm sandwich that makes an ideal lunch or supper dish.

1 small eggplant (1/2-3/4 lb. / 225-340g)
Olive oil
12 slices Italian or French bread or 6 hamburger buns, sliced
6 slices ham
6 slices Fontina or Gruyère cheese
1-2 teaspoons (5-10ml) dried oregano leaves
Mustard
6 Romaine lettuce leaves

Preheat broiler or grill. Cut eggplant into 1/4-inch (6mm) slices to fit bread. Brush both sides of eggplant with oil and broil or grill until tender. Remove and drain on paper towels.

Place eggplant slices on 6 bread slices or bottom of hamburger buns, cover with ham and cheese and sprinkle with oregano. Return to broiler or grill. Heat until cheese begins to melt.

Brush remaining bread slices or hamburger buns with mustard and cover with a lettuce leaf. Assemble sandwiches and serve at once.

Makes 6 servings.

Each serving contains:

Cal	Prot	Carb	Fib	Tot. Fat	Sat. Fat	Chol	Sodium
420	20g	37g	4g	21g	9g	54mg	1369mg

Sage-Béchamel Casserole

This recipe is quite rich, with just a hint of nutmeg. It calls for simple accompaniments.

1-1/2 lb. (700g) eggplant, cut into strips (1 x 2-inch / 2.5x5cm)
3 tablespoons (45ml) melted butter
Salt and pepper to taste
1 tablespoon (15ml) flour
1/2 cup (125ml) sour cream
1 cup (250ml) Béchamel Sauce, page 161
1 teaspoon (5ml) chopped chives
Dash of nutmeg
2 teaspoons (10ml) chopped sage leaves
1/2 cup (125ml) chopped smoked ham
1/2 cup (125ml) grated Gruyère cheese (2 oz. / 60g)

Preheat oven to 375F (190C). Lightly butter a shallow 9-inch-square (22.5cm) baking dish, or spray with vegetable cooking spray.

Cook eggplant strips in boiling water 5 to 7 minutes. Drain and pat dry with paper towels. Place in prepared baking dish, drizzle with butter and toss to coat. Season with salt and pepper.

Stir flour into sour cream. Add béchamel sauce, chives, nutmeg, sage and ham. Spoon over eggplant and sprinkle with cheese.

Bake 20 to 25 minutes, until tender.

Makes 6 servings.

Each serving contains:

Cal	Prot	Carb	Fib	Tot. Fat	Sat. Fat	Chol	Sodium
254	7g	13g	3g	19g	11g	55mg	302mg

Ham-Filled Eggplants

I Mirizan I Pieni
(Corsica)

An attractive and flavorful dish is complemented by a tomato sauce with a difference.

> *6 small Japanese eggplants, total weight 1-1/2 lb. (700g)*
> *Salt*
> *2 slices bread*
> *1 cup (250ml) milk*
> *1 cup (250ml) chopped ham*
> *1/4 cup (60ml) chopped fresh basil*
> *2 garlic cloves, minced*
> *1/2 cup (125ml) peas*
> *1/2 cup (125ml) grated Parmesan or brocciu cheese*
> *Pepper to taste*
> *Corsican Sauce, below*

Boil whole eggplants in salted water 5 to 6 minutes. Soak bread in milk.

Remove eggplants from water and cut in half lengthwise. Remove flesh with a spoon, leaving a 1/4-inch (6mm) layer next to skin. Preheat oven to 400F (200C).

Chop together ham, eggplant flesh, basil and garlic. Drain bread, squeezing to remove excess liquid, crumble and add to mixture. Add peas, cheese, salt and pepper.

Fill skins with stuffing and place in baking dish. Cover with sauce and bake 20 minutes.

Makes 6 servings.

Each serving contains:

Cal	Prot	Carb	Fib	Tot. Fat	Sat. Fat	Chol	Sodium
225	14g	22g	5g	9g	4g	25mg	728mg

Corsican Sauce

1 slice bacon, chopped
1 onion, chopped
2 garlic cloves, minced
1 tablespoon (15ml) oil
1 lb. (450g) tomatoes, peeled and chopped,
*   or 1 can (16-oz. / 450g) tomatoes*
1/4 cup (60ml) chopped fresh basil
Salt and pepper to taste

Sauté bacon, onion and garlic in hot oil. Add tomatoes, basil, salt and pepper. Simmer uncovered 15 minutes.

Makes 2-1/2 cups (625ml).

One serving contains:

Cal	Prot	Carb	Fib	Tot. Fat	Sat. Fat	Chol	Sodium
63	2g	6g	1g	4g	1g	3mg	103mg

Bacon-Wrapped Eggplants

Aubergines en Portefeuille au Jambon Cru

(Provence)

These unusual little bundles are packed with flavor.

6 small Japanese eggplants, total weight 1-1/2 lb. (700g)
2 tablespoons (30ml) parsley
4 garlic cloves, minced
3 thin slices ham, cut in half
Salt and pepper
6 slices bacon
6 sprigs rosemary
1/4 cup (60ml) olive oil

Remove stems and peel eggplants, leaving a few strips of skin. Make a slit lengthwise through each eggplant, being careful not to cut it in half. Open carefully and remove flesh from each side with a small spoon.

Combine eggplant flesh, parsley and garlic. Place a piece of ham and a little parsley mixture inside each eggplant. Season with salt and pepper. Close up eggplant and wrap each with a slice of bacon, "pinned" with a piece of rosemary.

In a heavy pan, heat oil and cook eggplants over high heat, turning several times. Reduce heat and simmer 20 to 30 minutes, until tender. Serve hot.

Makes 6 servings.

Each serving contains:

Cal	Prot	Carb	Fib	Tot. Fat	Sat. Fat	Chol	Sodium
181	6g	9g	3g	14g	3g	13mg	337mg

Eggplant with Bacon and Mushrooms

Dried mushrooms come in many sizes, shapes and varieties. If you've never cooked with them, this might be a good place to start.

1-1/2 lb. (700g) eggplant, cut crosswise into 1/4-inch (6mm) slices
Salt
6 dried mushrooms
2 tablespoons (30ml) olive oil
2 onions, chopped
2 garlic cloves, chopped
6 slices bacon, chopped
2 tomatoes, chopped
1 tablespoon (15ml) chopped parsley
Pepper to taste
Bouquet garni (bay leaf, thyme, parsley)

Sprinkle eggplant slices with salt and drain in colander 20 minutes. Pat dry with paper towels.

Soak mushrooms in a bowl of hot water 15 minutes. Drain, discard water and chop mushrooms.

In a Dutch oven or large skillet, heat oil and sauté onions, garlic and bacon. Add tomatoes, parsley, mushrooms, salt, pepper and bouquet garni and simmer 10 minutes Add eggplant, cover and simmer 30 minutes, stirring often. Discard bouquet garni.

Makes 6 servings.

Each serving contains:

Cal	Prot	Carb	Fib	Tot. Fat	Sat. Fat	Chol	Sodium
217	8g	16g	4g	14g	4g	16mg	359mg

Russian-Style Stuffed Eggplants

If there is stuffing left over, put it in a baking dish and cook along with the eggplant.

> *3 small eggplants, each 1/2 lb. (225g), cut in half lengthwise*
> *Salt*
> *1/2 lb. (340g) pork sausage*
> *1 onion, chopped*
> *1/4 lb. (115g) sliced fresh mushrooms*
> *1/2 cup (185ml) cooked rice*
> *Pepper to taste*
> *1/2 red bell pepper, chopped*
> *1 tablespoon (15ml) chopped dill*
> *Sour cream for garnish*

Oil a baking dish large enough to hold eggplant halves in a single layer. Remove flesh with a spoon, leaving a 1/4-inch (6mm) layer next to skin. Place shells, cut side up, in prepared dish. Chop flesh, sprinkle with salt and drain in colander 20 minutes. Pat dry with paper towels. Preheat oven to 400F (200C).

In a large skillet, cook sausage until brown. Add onion, eggplant and mushrooms and cook, stirring, about 5 minutes. Stir in rice, salt and pepper.

Spoon filling into eggplant shells and top with bell pepper and dill. Bake about 20 minutes. Serve topped with a dollop of sour cream.

Makes 6 servings.

Each serving contains:

Cal	Prot	Carb	Fib	Tot. Fat	Sat. Fat	Chol	Sodium
248	10g	16g	4g	16g	7g	40mg	549mg

Stuffed Eggplants from Provence

Aubergines Farcies au Porc et au Riz

A wonderful, warming dish for fall, when a chill nips the air.

1-1/2 lb. (700g) small eggplants, cut in half lengthwise.
Salt
5 tablespoons (75ml) olive oil
1/2 lb. (700g) pork sausage or ground beef
1 onion, chopped
2 garlic cloves, minced
2 tablespoons (30ml) parsley
1 teaspoon (5ml) dried thyme leaves
4 oz. (115g) fresh mushrooms, sliced
3 tomatoes, peeled and chopped
1/4 cup (60ml) pitted green olives
1 cup (250ml) cooked rice
2 eggs, beaten
1 cup (250ml) shredded Gruyère cheese (4 oz. / 115g)
Pepper to taste

Remove eggplant flesh with a spoon, leaving a l/4-inch (6mm) layer next to skin. Sprinkle skins and flesh with salt and drain in separate colanders 20 minutes. Pat dry with paper towels.

Heat 2 tablespoons (30ml) oil in a large skillet. Fry sausage or beef meat and onion together. Add garlic, parsley, thyme, mushrooms and tomatoes. Cook, uncovered, until mixture has thickened, add eggplant flesh and olives and cook 15 minutes. Preheat oven to 375F (190C).

Remove eggplant mixture from heat and add rice, eggs, cheese and salt and pepper to taste. Fill the eggplant skins with this mixture and arrange them in a baking dish. Pour remaining olive oil over the top and bake 30 minutes. Serve hot.

Makes 6 servings.

Each serving contains:

Cal	Prot	Carb	Fib	Tot. Fat	Sat. Fat	Chol	Sodium
447	18g	24g	4g	32g	10g	122mg	740mg

Italian Baked Eggplants with Sausage

This is like lasagna without the noodles. The flavors go well together.

3 small eggplants, each 1/2 lb. (225g), cut in half lengthwise
Salt
2 slices bread
1/2 cup (125ml) milk
1/2 lb. (225g) sweet Italian sausage meat
1 onion, chopped
1 cup (250ml) ricotta cheese
1/2 cup (125ml) grated Parmesan cheese
3 sun-dried tomato halves, drained and chopped
2 tablespoons (30ml) chopped basil
1 tablespoon (15ml) chopped parsley
1/2 cup (125ml) breadcrumbs
1 recipe Tomato Sauce, page 119

Place eggplant halves in boiling salted water for 10 minutes. Remove from water and drain. Remove and chop flesh, leaving a 1/4-inch (6mm) border around each half. Set aside. Place flesh in large bowl. Preheat oven to 375F (190C).Tear bread into pieces and soak in milk.

In a skillet, brown sausage, add onion and sauté. Add to eggplant. Drain bread, squeezing to remove excess liquid, crumble and add to mixture. Stir in ricotta and Parmesan cheeses, sun-dried tomatoes, basil, and parsley.

Place shells in a baking dish and fill with stuffing. Sprinkle tops with breadcrumbs. Bake about 25 minutes. Serve with tomato sauce.

Makes 6 servings.

Each serving contains:

Cal	Prot	Carb	Fib	Tot. Fat	Sat. Fat	Chol	Sodium
422	19g	34g	6g	24g	10g	58mg	932mg

Turkish Chicken

Patlicanli Pilic

Currants and pine nuts add texture as well as flavor.

> *1 lb. (450g) eggplant, cut crosswise into 1/2-inch (1.25cm) slices*
> *Salt*
> *Olive oil for brushing*
> *1 tablespoon (15ml) butter*
> *1 chicken, cut into pieces*
> *2 green bell peppers, seeded and cut into rings*
> *1 onion, sliced*
> *1-1/4 cups (310ml) chicken stock*
> *1 tablespoon (15ml) lemon juice*
> *2 tomatoes, cut into quarters*
> *2 tablespoons (30ml) dried currants*
> *2 tablespoons (30ml) pine nuts*
> *Pepper to taste*

Sprinkle eggplant slices with salt and drain in colander 20 minutes. Pat dry with paper towels. Preheat broiler or grill.

Brush or spray both sides of eggplant slices with oil, broil or grill until lightly browned. Remove and set aside on paper towels. Cut each slice into 6 pieces. Preheat oven to 360F (180C).

Heat butter and 3 tablespoons olive oil in a large skillet. Add chicken pieces and brown on all sides. Place chicken in a large baking dish. Cover with layers of eggplant, bell pepper and onion. Combine chicken stock and lemon juice and pour into dish. Add tomatoes, currants, pine nuts, salt and pepper to taste.

Bake 35 to 45 minutes until chicken is done.

Makes 6 servings.

Each serving contains:

Cal	Prot	Carb	Fib	Tot. Fat	Sat. Fat	Chol	Sodium
511	32g	13g	3g	37g	10g	120mg	340mg

Chicken and Eggplant

(Armenia)

The foods of Armenia, Turkey and Greece share a common heritage developed from the Byzantine and Ottoman cultures. Yogurt plays an important part in their cooking, and is often used as a topping, as in this recipe.

1 lb. (450g) eggplant, cubed
Salt
1/2 cup (125ml) all-purpose flour
1/2 teaspoon (2ml) paprika
1 teaspoon (5ml) dried basil leaves
1 chicken (2-1/2-lb. / 1.15kg), cut into pieces
3 tablespoons (45ml) oil
1 leek, sliced, white part only
1 garlic clove, chopped
3 tablespoons (45ml) chopped pimentos
6-8 green olives, sliced
1 cup (250ml) white wine
Salt and pepper to taste
Chopped parsley
Cooked rice
1/2 cup (125ml) plain yogurt
Dash of cinnamon
Dash of sugar

Sprinkle eggplant with salt and drain in colander 20 minutes. Pat dry with paper towels.

Place flour, paprika and basil in a paper or plastic bag. Add chicken pieces and toss to coat. Heat oil in Dutch oven or large skillet. Add chicken and brown on all sides. Stir in leek and garlic. Cook, stirring, until softened.

Add eggplant, pimentos, olives, wine, salt and pepper. Reduce heat, cover and simmer until chicken and eggplant are tender.

Combine yogurt, cinnamon and sugar.

Serve chicken over hot cooked rice. Sprinkle with parsley. Top with flavored yogurt.

Makes 6 servings.

Each serving contains:

Cal	Prot	Carb	Fib	Tot. Fat	Sat. Fat	Chol	Sodium
653	40g	32g	4g	38g	10g	144mg	367mg

Chicken and Penne

Penne, also known as *quill macaroni,* are long straight pasta tubes cut on the diagonal.

> *1-1/2 lb. (700g) eggplant, cut crosswise into 1/4-inch (6mm) slices*
> *Salt*
> *Oil*
> *Cooked penne pasta*
> *3 tomatoes, sliced*
> *1-1/2 cups (375ml) sliced cooked chicken*
> *Red pepper flakes (optional)*
> *Mushroom Sauce, below*

Sprinkle eggplant slices with salt and drain in colander 20 minutes. Pat dry with paper towels.

Preheat broiler or grill. Brush or spray both sides of eggplant slices with oil and broil or grill until tender.

Divide pasta among serving plates. Alternate tomato and eggplant slices on top. Pour mushroom sauce over and sprinkle with red pepper flakes, if using.

Makes 6 servings.

Each serving contains:

Cal	Prot	Carb	Fib	Tot. Fat	Sat. Fat	Chol	Sodium
436	19g	40g	5g	23g	8g	55mg	317mg

Mushroom Sauce

4 tablespoons (60ml) butter
1 tablespoon (15ml) olive oil
1/4 lb. (115g) sliced fresh mushrooms
2 green onions, chopped
3 tablespoons (45ml) all-purpose flour
3/4 cup (185ml) chicken broth
3/4 cup (185ml) milk or half-and-half
Salt and pepper to taste

In a saucepan heat 1 tablespoon (15ml) butter and oil. Cook mushrooms and onions until mushrooms are tender. Remove mixture and set aside. Add remaining butter to skillet and stir in flour, making a smooth paste. Stir in broth and half-and-half. Return mushrooms and onions to pan and heat through. Season with salt and pepper.

Makes 2 cups (500ml).

One serving contains:

Cal	Prot	Carb	Fib	Tot. Fat	Sat. Fat	Chol	Sodium
128	3g	6g	0g	11g	6g	23mg	236mg

Chicken Provençal

Poulet aux Aubergines Fagon Provençale

Thyme flavors the chicken from the inside in this one-dish meal.

1 lb. (450g) eggplant, cut crosswise into 1/2-inch (1.25cm) slices
Salt
1 chicken (2-1/2 lb. / 1kg)
Pepper to taste
10-12 sprigs fresh thyme, or 1 tablespoon dried thyme leaves
2 tablespoons (30ml) olive oil
1 tablespoon (15ml) butter
1 onion, chopped
1 tablespoon (15ml) tomato purée
1 cup (250ml) water
2 tomatoes, peeled, seeded and chopped
4 garlic cloves, crushed
1 bay leaf
Parsley for garnish

Sprinkle eggplant with salt and drain in colander 20 minutes. Pat dry with paper towels. Season inside of chicken with salt and pepper, and stuff it with thyme.

In a Dutch oven or large pot, heat oil and butter together; cook chicken until golden on all sides.

When chicken is ready, remove and set aside. Add eggplant slices to the pot and fry over high heat 5 minutes, stirring occasionally. Season with salt and pepper.

Add onion, tomato purée, water and tomatoes. Return chicken to pot and add garlic and bay leaf. Cover and simmer 35 to 45 minutes over low heat. Remove and discard bay leaf.

Serve chicken sprinkled with parsley and surrounded by vegetables.

Makes 6 servings.

Each serving contains:

Cal	Prot	Carb	Fib	Tot. Fat	Sat. Fat	Chol	Sodium
328	42g	10g	3g	13g	3g	137mg	229mg

Main Dishes with Seafood

From Fisherman's Surprise to Shrimp and Eggplant Kebabs, here are some unusual dishes to bring out when you are entertaining. Smoked salmon is an ingredient usually reserved for guests—it is featured in two recipes from Russia.

Prosciutto is the unexpected ingredient in Shrimp Gratin, while Crab, Spinach and Eggplant Crepes rise above the ordinary through the herbs added to the crepes.

Fisherman's Surprise

Lou Tian Souspresso di Pescadou de Sormiou
(Marseilles)

The surprise is the addition of eggplant to this tasty dish.

1-1/2 lb. (700g) eggplant, cut crosswise into 1/4-inch (6mm) slices
Salt
Oil for brushing
1 can (8-oz. / 225g) tomato sauce
6 thin sole fillets
1/4 teaspoon (1ml) garlic powder
2 tablespoons (30ml) chopped basil
3 tablespoons (45ml) olive oil
1/4 cup (60ml) lemon juice or white wine
3 tomatoes, peeled and chopped
Pepper to taste
1/2 cup (125ml) grated Gruyère cheese (2 oz. / 60g)

Preheat broiler. Sprinkle eggplant slices with salt and drain in colander 20 minutes. Pat dry with paper towels. Oil a baking sheet.

Brush or spray eggplant with oil and place on prepared baking sheet. Broil both sides until golden. Remove and drain on paper towels. Reduce oven temperature to 425F (220C).

Brush each eggplant slice with tomato sauce, place a fillet on top of sauce. Combine garlic powder, basil and olive oil and spread on fillets. Roll up and place seam side down in a greased baking dish. Pour lemon juice or wine into dish, scatter tomatoes on top and season to taste with pepper. Sprinkle with cheese and bake 10 to 15 minutes.

Makes 6 servings.

Each serving contains:

Cal	Prot	Carb	Fib	Tot. Fat	Sat. Fat	Chol	Sodium
388	35g	13g	4g	21g	4g	88mg	445mg

Veracruz Eggplant with Cod
(Mexico)

Olives give this dish its special flavor. The recipe works well with any kind of firm whitefish.

1 lb. (450g) eggplant, peeled and cut into cubes
2 tablespoons (30ml) lemon juice
1 lb. (450g) cod fillets, cut into 1-1/2-inch (3.75cm) cubes
3 tablespoons (45ml) oil
1 onion, sliced
2 garlic cloves, chopped
1 red bell pepper, cut into strips
1 can (8-oz. / 225g) tomato sauce
1 tablespoon (15ml) chopped cilantro
1 can (4-oz. / 115g) peeled chile pepper, chopped
1/2 cup (125ml) sliced pimento-stuffed olives
1 tablespoon (15ml) capers

Sprinkle eggplant cubes with salt and drain in colander 20 minutes. Pat dry with paper towels. Place lemon juice in a bowl, add cod, toss to coat and set aside.

In a Dutch oven or large skillet heat oil and sauté onion and garlic. Add eggplant, bell pepper, tomato sauce and cilantro. Cover and simmer 25 minutes.

Add cod with lemon juice, chile pepper and olives. Cover and cook over medium heat 7 to 10 minutes.

Makes 6 servings.

Each serving contains:

Cal	Prot	Carb	Fib	Tot. Fat	Sat. Fat	Chol	Sodium
190	16g	15g	4g	9g	1g	33mg	417mg

Eggplant with Salmon in Cream
(Russia)

An elegant dish that is easy to prepare. Your guests will love it.

1-1/2 lb. (700g) eggplant, cut crosswise into thin slices
Salt
Oil for frying
1/4 lb. (115g) smoked salmon, thinly sliced
Pepper
1 cup (250ml) sour cream
1 tablespoon (15ml) chopped chives

Sprinkle eggplant slices with salt and drain in colander 20 minutes. Pat dry with paper towels. Preheat oven to 425F (220C). Grease a baking dish. Heat oil in large skillet.

Fry eggplant slices quickly in hot oil and drain in colander or on paper towels.

Place eggplant slices in prepared baking dish, cover with salmon, season with pepper and top with sour cream. Sprinkle with chives. Bake in oven 15 minutes. Serve hot.

Makes 6 servings.

Each serving contains:

Cal	Prot	Carb	Fib	Tot. Fat	Sat. Fat	Chol	Sodium
216	6g	9g	3g	18g	6g	21mg	216mg

Salmon-Topped Eggplant

(Russia)

Capers are dried flower buds of a bush that is native to the Mediterranean and parts of Asia. They are usually packed in brine, so rinse before using to remove excess salt.

1-1/2 lb. (700g) eggplant, cut crosswise into 1/4-inch (6mm) slices
1 tablespoon (15ml) sunflower oil
3 slices of bread, crusts removed
1 cup (250ml) milk
3 eggs, beaten
2 tablespoons (30ml) capers
2 green onions, chopped
1/4 teaspoon (1ml) garlic powder
Salt and pepper to taste
3 oz. (85g) smoked salmon
1 cup (250ml) grated Edam or Gouda cheese (4 oz. / 115g)

Preheat oven to 350F (175C). Brush eggplant slices lightly with oil and place on a baking sheet. Bake 20 minutes.

Soak bread slices in milk and then squeeze dry. Crumble and combine with eggs, capers, green onions, garlic powder, salt and pepper.

Top eggplant with salmon and cover salmon with the stuffing. Sprinkle with grated cheese. Return to oven for 10 minutes.

Makes 6 servings.

Each serving contains:

Cal	Prot	Carb	Fib	Tot. Fat	Sat. Fat	Chol	Sodium
252	15g	19g	3g	13g	6g	133mg	610mg

Shrimp Gratin

(Catalan)

This is good over rice or noodles or, for a change, baked potatoes.

1-1/2 lb. (700g) eggplant, unpeeled
1/2 lb. (200g) cooked, shelled shrimp
7 oz. (200g) prosciutto, cubed
Béchamel Sauce, below
1-3/4 cups (440ml) grated Parmesan or Gruyère cheese
(7 oz. / 200g)

Preheat oven to 400F (200C). Grease a baking dish. Blanch whole eggplants in boiling water 10 minutes. Cut into small cubes.

Place eggplant, shrimp and prosciutto in prepared baking dish. Top with béchamel sauce and sprinkle with grated cheese. Bake in oven 20 minutes. Serve hot.

Makes 6 servings.

Each serving contains:

Cal	Prot	Carb	Fib	Tot. Fat	Sat. Fat	Chol	Sodium
317	27g	13g	3g	17g	10g	108mg	1062mg

Béchamel Sauce

2 tablespoons (30ml) butter
2 tablespoons (30ml) flour
1 cup (250ml) milk

Melt butter over low heat. Sprinkle in flour, stirring constantly. Pour milk in all at once and cook gently, stirring constantly, until sauce is thick. Remove from heat.

Makes 1 cup (250ml).

One serving contains:

Cal	Prot	Carb	Fib	Tot. Fat	Sat. Fat	Chol	Sodium
64	2g	4g	0g	5g	3g	13mg	59mg

Crab, Spinach and Eggplant Crepes

These can be made early in the day and refrigerated. Heat, covered, in a 350F (175C) oven until crepes are hot and cheese is melted.

8 Herb Crepes, below
1/2 lb. (225g) eggplant, peeled and cubed
4 green onions, chopped
3 tablespoons (45ml) butter
3 tablespoons (45ml) all-purpose flour
3/4 cup (185ml) milk
1/2 cup (125ml) dry vermouth
1 pkg. (10-oz. / 280g) frozen spinach, thawed and drained
3/4 cup (185ml) crab meat (6 oz. / 170g)
1 cup (250ml) shredded mozzarella or Swiss cheese (4 oz. / 115g)

Sprinkle eggplant with salt and drain in colander 20 minutes. Pat dry with paper towels. Boil eggplant in water to cover about 7 minutes. Drain and set aside. Preheat oven to 350F (175C).

In a large skillet, melt butter and sauté onions. Stir in flour, making a smooth paste. Stir in milk and vermouth. Cook until blended and slightly thickened. Stir in eggplant, spinach and crab.

Place 1 tablespoon (15ml) cheese on each crepe, top with filling and roll up. Place, seam side down, in a baking dish. Sprinkle remaining cheese over filled crepes. Bake uncovered about 20 minutes, until heated through.

Makes 4 servings.

Each serving contains:

Cal	Prot	Carb	Fib	Tot. Fat	Sat. Fat	Chol	Sodium
510	23g	44g	5g	24g	14g	193mg	497mg

Herb Crepes

2 eggs
1 cup (250ml) milk
1 cup (250ml) all-purpose flour
1/2 teaspoon (2ml) dried tarragon leaves
1/2 teaspoon (2ml) dried thyme leaves
1 tablespoon (15ml) melted butter or oil
Salt and pepper to taste

Beat eggs in a bowl or blender. Add remaining ingredients. Let batter rest while eggplant drains.

Heat a small skillet or crepe pan. Lightly coat with vegetable-oil spray. Pour in 1/4 cup (60ml) batter. Swirl batter to cover bottom of pan. When edges curl and begin to brown, turn crepe and cook other side about 1 minute. Cover and keep warm. Repeat with remaining batter.

Makes 8 crepes.

One serving contains:

Cal	Prot	Carb	Fib	Tot. Fat	Sat. Fat	Chol	Sodium
208	8g	27g	1g	7g	3g	119mg	159mg

Shrimp and Eggplant Kebabs

(United States)

Use 10-inch skewers when making this summertime meal-on-a-stick.

1 lb. (450g) eggplant, peeled and cubed
Barbecue Sauce, below
3/4 lb. (340g) shrimp, peeled (about 18 shrimp)
6 oz. (170g) fresh whole button mushrooms
1 large green bell pepper, cut into 1-inch (2.5cm) squares
12 cherry tomatoes

Sprinkle eggplant with salt and drain in colander 20 minutes. Pat dry with paper towels.

Add eggplant cubes and shrimp to cooled barbecue sauce. Toss to coat and let stand in marinade at least 30 minutes. Preheat grill or broiler.

Thread alternating pieces of eggplant, shrimp, mushrooms, bell pepper and tomatoes onto long skewers. Brush with sauce.

Place on grill or broiler pan and brush again with sauce. Cook 3-4 minutes on each side, brushing kebabs with sauce several times.

Makes 6 servings.

Each serving contains:

Cal	Prot	Carb	Fib	Tot. Fat	Sat. Fat	Chol	Sodium
285	15g	34g	5g	12g	2g	111mg	824mg

Barbecue Sauce

3 tablespoons (45ml) oil
1 onion, chopped
6 tablespoons (95ml) brown sugar
6 tablespoons (95ml) lime juice or vinegar
1 teaspoon (5ml) dry mustard
2 cans (8-oz. / 225g) tomato sauce
1/2 teaspoon (2ml) garlic powder
1/2 cup (125ml) water
Dash of allspice

Heat oil in saucepan and sauté onion until golden. Add remaining ingredients and simmer about 15 minutes. Set aside to cool.

Makes 2-1/2 to 3 cups.

One serving contains:

Cal	Prot	Carb	Fib	Tot. Fat	Sat. Fat	Chol	Sodium
131	1g	18g	1g	7g	1g	0mg	462mg

Sicilian-Style Eggplants with Sardines
Melanzana Imbottite alla Siciliana

You could eat sardines right out of the can. Or, use them to make this rich, cheese-topped dish.

Oil for frying
3 long eggplants, each 1/2 lb. (225g), cut in half lengthwise
1 onion, chopped
1 garlic clove, minced
Salt and pepper to taste
1 can (3.75 oz. / 106g) sardines in oil, drained
2 tablespoons (30ml) capers
1 teaspoon (5ml) sage leaves
3-1/2 oz. (100g) soft goat cheese or fresh mozzarella, cut
*   into 6 slices*
Seasoned breadcrumbs for topping

Heat oil in a deep skillet. Deep-fry eggplants until golden. Remove with a slotted spoon and drain. Remove flesh with a spoon, leaving a 1/4-inch (6mm) layer next to skin. Roughly chop eggplant flesh. Preheat oven to 425F (220C). Grease a large baking dish.

Heat a little oil in a pan and cook onion and garlic until onion is transparent. Add eggplant. Season with salt and pepper and cook 15 minutes over low heat, stirring occasionally. Mash sardines and add to eggplant mixture. Mix well. Add capers, sage and 1 tablespoon oil.

Fill eggplant skins with mixture; cover with cheese. Arrange eggplants on prepared baking dish; top with breadcrumbs. Bake 20 to 30 minutes.

Makes 6 servings.

Each serving contains:

Cal	Prot	Carb	Fib	Tot. Fat	Sat. Fat	Chol	Sodium
219	10g	13g	3g	15g	4g	38mg	341mg

Main Dishes
with Eggs

$\mathcal{E}$ggs and eggplant may not seem like a natural combination, but the recipes in this chapter prove that they go very well together.

Offered are a variety of omelets, such as Baked Tomato-Cheese Omelet and Cheese and Eggplant Omelet. Greek Quiche with Three Cheeses introduces a different flavor, with Myzithra cheese leading the way.

Try Mexican Eggs and Eggplant for hearty brunch or luncheon fare.

Eggplant Quiche

Serve this quiche with a tomato sauce on the side, and accompanied by a green salad with an olive oil and lemon juice dressing.

1 lb. (450g) eggplant, cubed
Salt
3 tablespoons (45ml) olive oil
4 chopped shallots or green onions
Pinch of thyme
Pepper to taste
4 eggs, beaten
4 pieces crisp cooked bacon, crumbled
3/4 cup (185ml) milk
3/4 cup (185ml) cream
1 cup (250ml) grated Swiss cheese (4 oz. / 115g)
1/2 cup (125ml) grated Parmesan cheese (2 oz. / 60g)
Tart pastry, page 36

Sprinkle eggplant with salt and drain in colander 20 minutes. Preheat oven to 400F (200C). Grease a tart pan. Dry eggplant with a paper towel and sauté in hot oil. Add chopped shallots or green onions, thyme and pepper. Set aside to cool.

Combine eggs, bacon, milk and cream and season with salt and pepper. Combine Swiss cheese and Parmesan cheese.

Line prepared tart pan with pastry and prick pastry with a fork. Spread eggplant mixture over crust, pour in egg mixture and sprinkle with mixed cheeses. Place in oven and bake 30 minutes. Serve warm.

Makes 6 servings.

Each serving contains:

Cal	Prot	Carb	Fib	Tot. Fat	Sat. Fat	Chol	Sodium
777	25g	42g	3g	57g	29g	309mg	786mg

Baked Eggplant with Eggs

This unusual combination is surprisingly good.

1 lb. (450g) eggplant
Juice of 1 lemon
2 tablespoons (30ml) olive oil or sour cream
1 tablespoon (15ml) ground mixed spices (nutmeg, cumin,
*   coriander, ginger)*
Salt and pepper
6 eggs

Preheat oven to 425F (220C). Prepare eggplant according to the basic caviar recipe, page 6. Mash flesh with a fork. Add lemon juice. Stirring constantly, add olive oil or sour cream, spices, salt and pepper. Set aside a quarter of the mixture.

Divide remaining mixture among 6 individual earthenware dishes. Using a small spoon, make a hole in the center of each dish. Break an egg into each hole. Cover egg with some of the reserved mixture and cover dishes with foil. Bake 15 minutes. Serve hot.

Makes 6 servings.

Each serving contains:

Cal	Prot	Carb	Fib	Tot. Fat	Sat. Fat	Chol	Sodium
141	7g	7g	2g	10g	2g	213mg	110mg

Herbed Eggplant Soufflé

(Armenia)

This is best made with fresh herbs. Use less if your herbs are dried.

1 lb. (450g) eggplant
6 eggs, beaten
1 teaspoon (5ml) Dijon-style mustard
2 tablespoons (30ml) chopped parsley
1 tablespoon (15ml) chopped tarragon
Salt and pepper
1/4 cup (60ml) grated Cheddar cheese
1 tablespoon (15ml) fine breadcrumbs

Prepare eggplant according to the basic caviar recipe, page 6. Mash the flesh roughly with a fork. Preheat oven to 400F (200C).

Fold eggplant flesh into beaten eggs. Add mustard, parsley, tarragon, salt, pepper and cheese.

Grease a soufflé dish. Sprinkle bottom of soufflé dish with breadcrumbs and pour in the mixture. Cook in oven 15 minutes.

Makes 6 servings.

Each serving contains:

Cal	Prot	Carb	Fib	Tot. Fat	Sat. Fat	Chol	Sodium
123	8g	7g	2g	7g	3g	217mg	170mg

Ratatouille Omelet

Omelette à la Ratatouille
(Provence)

A wonderful way to use leftovers.

1 cup (250ml) well-drained ratatouille, page 94
12 eggs, beaten
Salt and pepper
2 tablespoons (30ml) butter
Cooking oil
2 tablespoon (30ml) chopped black olives
1 tablespoon (15ml) chopped chives

Heat ratatouille very gently. Season beaten eggs with salt and pepper.

Heat butter and oil in a large skillet. Pour in eggs, olives and chives. When omelet is nearly ready, pour ratatouille onto one side of the omelet and fold the other half over.

Slip onto a hot plate and serve.

Makes 6 servings.

Variation
Beat eggs together and add remaining ingredients before cooking Cook omelet normally. Prepared this way, the omelet can be eaten cold and makes a delicious dish for a picnic.

Each serving contains:

Cal	Prot	Carb	Fib	Tot. Fat	Sat. Fat	Chol	Sodium
232	13g	3g	0g	19g	6g	435mg	192mg

Baked Tomato-Cheese Omelet

If you're concerned about cholesterol, feel free to use an egg substitute for the recipes in this chapter.

> *1 lb. (450g) eggplant, cut crosswise into 1/4-inch (6mm) slices*
> *Salt*
> *Oil*
> *4 tablespoons (60ml) butter*
> *3 tomatoes, sliced*
> *5 oz. (145g) mozzarella cheese, sliced*
> *8 eggs, beaten*
> *1 tablespoon (15ml) chopped basil*
> *Pepper*
> *2 tablespoons (30ml) chopped parsley*

Sprinkle eggplant slices with salt and drain in colander 20 minutes. Pat dry with paper towels. Preheat broiler. Grease a baking sheet.

Brush or spray eggplant with oil and place on prepared baking sheet. Broil both sides until golden. Remove and drain on paper towels. Reduce oven temperature to 325F (160C).

Melt butter with 2 tablespoons (30ml) oil in a large baking dish. Alternate overlapping slices of eggplant, tomato and cheese. Combine eggs, basil and pepper to taste. Pour over vegetables and cheese, sprinkle with parsley and bake about 30 minutes, until eggs are set as desired.

Makes 6 servings.

Each serving contains:

Cal	Prot	Carb	Fib	Tot. Fat	Sat. Fat	Chol	Sodium
308	14g	9g	3g	24g	11g	323mg	303mg

Mexican Eggs and Eggplant

Here's a refreshing version of the Mexican classic, *huevos rancheros.*

1 lb. (450g) eggplant, peeled and cubed
Salt
3 tablespoons (45ml) oil
1 onion, chopped
1 can (4-oz. / 115g) roasted chile peppers, drained and chopped
1 green bell pepper, chopped
4 tomatoes, chopped
1 can (8-oz. / 225g) tomato sauce
2 tablespoons (30ml) chopped cilantro leaves
1 teaspoon (5ml) dried oregano leaves
12 eggs
6 flour tortillas
1/2 cup (125ml) shredded Monterey Jack cheese (2 oz. / 60g)

Sprinkle eggplant with salt and drain in colander 20 minutes. Pat dry with paper towels.

In a large skillet heat butter and sauté onions. Add eggplant, peppers, tomatoes, tomato sauce, cilantro and oregano. Cover and simmer 20 minutes.

Make 12 indentations in sauce and break an egg into each. Cover and cook 3 to 5 minutes until eggs are done as desired. Top with cheese.

Warm tortillas and place one on each plate. Carefully spoon 2 eggs with sauce on each tortilla. Top with any remaining sauce.

Makes 6 servings.

Each serving contains:

Cal	Prot	Carb	Fib	Tot. Fat	Sat. Fat	Chol	Sodium
426	20g	37g	5g	23g	6g	433mg	631mg

Greek Quiche with Three Cheeses

Myzithra is a semi-hard Greek cheese. It is combined with feta and mozzarella in this elegant quiche.

Filling:
1-1/2 lb. (700g) eggplant, cut crosswise into 1/2-inch (1.25cm)
slices
Oil
3 eggs, separated
10 oz. (280g) feta cheese
2 tablespoons (30ml) flour
1/2 cup (125ml) grated Myzithra or Swiss cheese (2 oz. / 60g)
1 tablespoon (15ml) chopped oregano leaves
2 garlic cloves, crushed
Salt and pepper
3 oz. (85g) mozzarella cheese, sliced

Pastry:
1 cup (250ml) flour
6 tablespoons (90ml) butter, diced
2 tablespoons (30ml) water

Preheat oven to 375F (190C). Grease a cookie sheet and a quiche pan. Lay eggplant slices on prepared sheet; brush or spray with oil. Put in oven and bake 15 minutes, turning slices after 10 minutes.

Combine egg yolks, feta cheese, 2 tablespoons (30ml) flour, grated cheese, oregano and garlic. Season with salt and pepper and beat until mixture is smooth. Beat egg whites until stiff and fold into cheese mixture.

Make pastry: Place 1 cup (250ml) flour, a pinch of salt and butter in a bowl. Mix together with fingertips, working quickly. Gradually add water and continue to mix. Make a ball with the dough, roll out and line prepared quiche pan.

Arrange half the eggplant slices on pastry. Add egg-cheese mixture and cover with remaining eggplant. Bake in oven about 1 hour. Top with mozzarella slices and cook another 10 minutes.

Serve immediately.

Makes 6 servings.

Each serving contains:

Cal	Prot	Carb	Fib	Tot. Fat	Sat. Fat	Chol	Sodium
529	18g	29g	4g	39g	19g	198mg	857mg

Cheese and Eggplant Omelet

Experiment with other herb-and-vegetable combinations in this simple but tasty dish.

> *1-1/2 lb. (700g) eggplant, cut into 1/2-inch (1.25cm) cubes*
> *Salt*
> *2 tablespoons (30ml) oil*
> *1 small zucchini, sliced*
> *1 tablespoon (15ml) chopped parsley*
> *1 teaspoon (5ml) thyme or mint*
> *3 eggs, beaten*
> *Pepper*
> *1-3/4 cups (440ml) grated Swiss cheese (7 oz. / 200g)*

Sprinkle eggplant cubes with salt and drain in colander 20 minutes. Pat dry with paper towels.

Heat oil and sauté eggplant and zucchini. Sprinkle with parsley and thyme or mint, reduce heat, cover and simmer until tender.

Season eggs with salt and pepper and pour over eggplant. Top with cheese. Cover and cook until eggs are set and cheese is melted.

Makes 6 servings.

Each serving contains:

Cal	Prot	Carb	Fib	Tot. Fat	Sat. Fat	Chol	Sodium
232	13g	10g	3g	16g	7g	135mg	162mg

Pickles and Preserves

*I*n preparing these recipes, choose the best quality small or medium-sized oblong eggplants, ones that are very fresh, preferably firm, with smooth, shiny skins. They can be served cut into small pieces as snacks for aperitifs, or as accompaniments for cold meats, roast chicken or a pot-au-feu. Eggplant prepared in this way will give an original touch to a quick meal.

Indian Eggplant Pickle

This is a relatively unknown dish, but you may find it in Indian restaurants or specialty stores. If you find very firm eggplants, try this pickle—it keeps for months.

1-1/4 lb. (575g) eggplant, peeled and cut into cubes
Salt
1 cup (250ml) sesame oil
4 garlic cloves, minced
1 piece (2-inch / 5cm) fresh ginger
1 teaspoon (5ml) ground turmeric
6 small dried red chile peppers
4 bay leaves
2 teaspoons (10ml) mustard seeds
1 teaspoon (5ml) cumin seed
2 tablespoons (30ml) salt
1/4 cup (60ml) honey

Sprinkle eggplant cubes with salt and drain in colander 20 minutes. Pat dry with paper towels.

Heat 1/2 cup (125ml) oil in skillet and fry eggplant until golden. Remove and drain on paper towels, then place in a bowl.

Heat remaining oil and sauté garlic and ginger. Add remaining ingredients except honey. Cook 2 to 3 minutes, remove from heat and add honey. Pour over eggplant and toss well to coat.

Transfer to hot sterilized jars and seal. Set aside to ripen for one month. Remove and discard bay leaves before using.

Makes 2 pints.

1 tablespoon (15ml) contains:

Cal	Prot	Carb	Fib	Tot. Fat	Sat. Fat	Chol	Sodium
39	0g	2g	0g	4g	0g	0mg	206mg

Eggplant Confit
Aubergines Confites

This method of preservation is popular with those who do French cooking.

2 lb. (900g) eggplant, unpeeled
Salt
3 garlic bulbs (45 cloves), peeled
Fresh savory or rosemary sprigs
2 bay leaves
Dried red chile pepper flakes (optional)
Olive oil

Cut eggplant into 1/4-inch (6mm) slices. Sprinkle with salt and drain in colander 4 to 5 hours. Pat dry with paper towels.

In a crock or large jar, layer eggplant slices with garlic, savory or rosemary, bay leaves and chile pepper, if using. Cover with oil. Place a plate on top, ensuring the vegetables are packed tightly and immersed in oil. Cover and place in a cool, dark place or refrigerate.

Makes about 2 pints (1 liter).

1 tablespoon (15ml) contains:

Cal	Prot	Carb	Fib	Tot. Fat	Sat. Fat	Chol	Sodium
14	0g	2g	0g	1g	0g	0mg	5mg

Sweet and Sour Chutney

Eggplant blends well with contrasting flavor and textures.

1 lb. (450g) eggplant, peeled and cubed (4 cups / 1 liter)
Salt
1 green bell pepper
3 cups (750ml) chopped onions or leeks
2 carrots, chopped
1 celery rib, chopped
1 apple, seeded, chopped
3 tomatoes, seeded, chopped
1/2 cup (125ml) currants or raisins
1/2 teaspoon (2ml) paprika
1/2 teaspoon (2ml) ground allspice
1/4 teaspoon (1ml) cayenne pepper
2 cups (500ml) vinegar
3 cups (750ml) sugar

Sprinkle eggplant with salt and drain in colander 20 minutes. Pat dry with paper towels.

In a large pot, combine all ingredients except sugar and bring to a boil. Reduce heat, cover and simmer about 40 minutes. Add sugar and cook uncovered about 20 minutes, stirring occasionally, until thickened to desired consistency.

Spoon into hot sterilized jars and cover. Let cool and store in refrigerator. It will keep for weeks.

Makes 3-1/2 pints (1.75 liters).

1 tablespoon (15ml) contains:

Cal	Prot	Carb	Fib	Tot. Fat	Sat. Fat	Chol	Sodium
27	0g	8g	0g	0g	0g	0mg	4mg

Eggplant Jam

("Pied-Noir" Cuisine)

If you do not peel the eggplants this becomes a much blacker jam.

2 lb. (900g) eggplant, peeled and cut into cubes
6 cups (1.5 liters) sugar (2 lb. / 900g)
1-1/2 cups (375ml) water
1 teaspoon (5ml) grated fresh ginger
2 tablespoons (30ml) honey
1 tablespoon (15ml) lemon juice.
2 tablespoons (30ml) sesame seeds

Cut eggplant into cubes. Drop into boiling water and cook
10 minutes. Drain in colander, pressing cubes to remove excess juice.

In a large pan, heat sugar in 1-1/2 cups (375ml) water until dissolved.
Add eggplant and cook, stirring occasionally, until jam thickens. Skim
off any foam. Add ginger, honey, lemon juice and sesame seeds and
cook, stirring constantly, 2 minutes longer.

Pour into hot sterilized jars and seal.
Makes 3 to 4 pints (750 to 1000ml).

1 tablespoon (15ml) contains:

Cal	Prot	Carb	Fib	Tot. Fat	Sat. Fat	Chol	Sodium
53	0g	14g	0g	0g	0g	0mg	1mg

Armenian Preserves

The ultimate gourmet touch is to cut the eggplants down one side and stuff with peeled blanched almonds or shelled walnuts.

> *2 lb. (900g) tiny eggplants*
> *6 cups (1.5 liters) sugar (2 lb. / 900g)*
> *Whole cloves*
> *Juice of 1/2 lemon*

Drop eggplants into boiling water and cook 10 minutes. Drain in colander, pressing eggplants to remove excess juice. Place eggplants and sugar in a large pan. Cover and let stand overnight.

Add cloves and cook uncovered, without adding sugar, for 30 minutes until sugar is dissolved. Do not stir during this time, or sugar may crystallize. When syrup is golden, add lemon juice.

Pour into hot sterilized jars and seal.

Makes 3 to 4 pints (750 to 1000ml).

1 tablespoon (15ml) contains:

Cal	Prot	Carb	Fib	Tot. Fat	Sat. Fat	Chol	Sodium
51	0g	13g	0g	0g	0g	0mg	0mg

Bibliography

Dawson, Jeff. "Choosing and Using Varieties of Eggplant." *Fine Cooking,* vol. 16 (August/September 1996): pp.14-15.

de Candolle, A. *Origine des plantes cultivées.* Paris: Laffitte Reprints, 1883.

de Grace and Mordant de Launay. *L'Amanach du bon jardinier.* Paris: Audot, 1818.

Dosti, Rose. *Middle Eastern Cooking.* Tucson, AZ: HPBooks, 1982.

Henri Baillon. *Dictionnaire de botanique.* Hachette, 1876-1892.

Herbst, Sharon Tyler. *The Food Lover's Tiptionary.* New York: Hearst Books, 1994.

Herbst, Sharon Tyler. *The New Food Lover's Companion, 2nd edition.* Hauppauge, NY: Barron's Educational Series, Inc., 1995.

Johnson, Elaine. "Not just any eggplant." *Sunset,* vol. 197 (August 1996): pp. 120-123

Klein, Ernest. *English Etymological Dictionary.* New York: Elsevier Publishing Company.

Li-Hui-Lin. "Vegetables of Ancient China." *Economic Botany,* 1969, vol. 23, pp. 253-260.

Robinson, Kathleen and Pete Luckett. *Vegetarian's A to Z Guide to Fruits and Vegetables.* Tucon, AZ: Fisher Books, 1996.

Vercier, J. "Culture potagère." *Encyclopédie des sciences agricoles,* Hachette.

von Welanetz, Diana and Paul. *The Von Welanetz Guide to Ethnic Ingredients.* New York: Warner Books, Inc., 1982.

Index

Index of Foreign Titles